Motor
Girls

Motor
Girls

How Women Took the Wheel and Drove Boldly
Into the Twentieth Century

SUE MACY

FOREWORD BY DANICA PATRICK

NATIONAL GEOGRAPHIC

WASHINGTON, D.C.

To Nancy Laties Feresten, for driving me forward

Copyright © 2017 Sue Macy

All rights reserved. Reproduction of the whole or any part of the contents without written permission from the publisher is prohibited.

Since 1888, the National Geographic Society has funded more than 12,000 research, exploration, and preservation projects around the world. The Society receives funds from National Geographic Partners LLC, funded in part by your purchase. A portion of the proceeds from this book supports this vital work. To learn more, visit www.natgeo.com/info.

For more information, visit nationalgeographic.com, call 1-800-647-5463, or write to the following address:

National Geographic Partners
1145 17th Street N.W.
Washington, D.C. 20036-4688 U.S.A.

Visit us online at nationalgeographic.com/books

For librarians and teachers: ngchildrensbooks.org

More for kids from National Geographic:
kids.nationalgeographic.com

For information about special discounts for bulk purchases, please contact National Geographic Books Special Sales: ngspecsales@ngs.org

For rights or permissions inquiries, please contact National Geographic Books Subsidiary Rights: ngbookrights@ngs.org

NATIONAL GEOGRAPHIC and Yellow Border Design are trademarks of the National Geographic Society, used under license.

Library of Congress Cataloging-in-Publication Data
Names: Macy, Sue.
Title: Motor girls : how women took the wheel and drove boldly into the twentieth century / by Sue Macy.
Description: Washington, D.C. : National Geographic Partners, [2016] |
    Includes bibliographical references and index.
Identifiers: LCCN 2016027123| ISBN 9781426326974 (hard cover : alk. paper) | ISBN 9781426326981 (library binding : alk. paper)
Subjects: LCSH: Women automobile drivers--Biography. | Automobile travel—History—20th century. | Automobiles—United States—History.
Classification: LCC TL139 .M33 2016 | DDC 629.28/309252 [B] —dc23

Printed in Hong Kong
16/THK/1

CONTENTS

Dust jacket: front cover, top: **Pioneer motorist Alice Ramsey takes the wheel during her 1909 drive across the United States. She won the bronze medal on her cap by getting a perfect score in an endurance race in New York.** *Bottom:* **Ramsey and her three companions in their Maxwell automobile on a rural dirt road;** *Back cover:* **Joan Newton Cuneo drives through Saratoga Springs, New York, during the 1908 Glidden endurance race.** *Front flap:* **Alice Ramsey and her passengers in 1909**

Case cover: **In 1909 four women in a Jackson-brand automobile show participants in the Glidden endurance race the way to Jackson, Michigan.**

Half-title page: **A woman shows off her car in 1908.**

Title page: **In this 1910 publicity shot for the Mercer motor car, a woman peers off into the future.**

Left: **Irene Wright gets a preview of a 1912 model at the Chalmers automobile factory in Detroit, Michigan.**

Foreword
BY DANICA PATRICK

When I was growing up, my parents never so much as hinted that my future could be determined by the fact that I was a girl. My mom had been a mechanic, and my dad loved to race all kinds of vehicles, and they both nurtured my own interest in racing. My dad always told me: "Don't be the best girl, be the best driver." And that has always stuck with me.

I began racing go-karts when I was 10 years old. When I was 16, I made the decision to pursue my passion for driving and moved to England to enter the competitive world of European road racing. At the time, despite incredible advances made by the original female racers and later pioneers like Janet Guthrie and Lyn St. James, it was still pretty rare for women to race either in Europe or back home in the United States. But I wasn't focused on that. I just wanted to drive—fast.

I eventually came back home and raced my way up to the IndyCar Series ranks, where I became the first female driver to lead the Indy 500 in 2005. Three years later, I became the first woman to win an IndyCar race when I took the checkered flag in the Indy Japan 300 at Twin Ring Motegi. I later made the transition to stock cars and ended up winning the pole for the 2013 Daytona 500.

Given how far I've made it in my career, it's hard to believe that up until the early 1970s women weren't even allowed in the pits during races in the IndyCar

❝ I think you have to feel comfortable with your car. You have to go into turn one, every lap, with confidence. You have to be sure of yourself and your equipment.”
—Danica Patrick, "Indianapolis 500 Press Conference," motorsport.com, May 19, 2011

Series. And despite the miles we have covered since then, I know there are some who still think that racing isn't meant for women.

In the future I want to be remembered as a great race car driver with terrific accomplishments, and not just as a "girl driver." Women have covered impressive distances since the Motor Girls first made history, but they still often face unexpected hurdles or extra scrutiny. Throughout it all you have to remember to stay true to yourself and what you believe, and use those who discourage you as motivation to become better.

And always remember this: You are never less qualified or competent because of your differences. The world is full of varied and unique people. I have always felt that it is important to make my own path in life—not to follow in someone else's footsteps and become another version of them, but rather to be the very first me. There are so many ways to use your talents and so many ways to make a career out of whatever you're interested in. I encourage you to embrace being different, and to become the very first **you** the world has ever seen.

Above: Danica Patrick is suited up in January 2016, her 15th year racing automobiles in the United States. As a teenager, she won the World Karting Association Grand National Championship three times.

Introduction
SUE MACY

My first car was a small, clunky, black 1964 Ford Falcon that my dad bought in 1972 so I could commute to my summer job as a newspaper reporter. It smelled kind of musty and was stripped down inside, and I never quite felt the connection I would have to my future automobiles. But I vividly remember driving to and from work, blasting "Take Me Home, Country Roads" and other John Denver tunes on the (AM-only) radio, feeling the power of the endless possibilities that lay before me that summer of my 18th year.

Automobiles can do that to you. When you're at the wheel, you're literally driving into the future, even if you're in a used, no-frills Ford Falcon. Cars are more than the sum of the metal, rubber, and plastic parts that go into them. They're vehicles for growth and change and an integral part of the rites of passage we experience throughout our lives. First car, snazzy car, family car, dependable car. As our situations change, our automobiles change with them.

At the end of the nineteenth century, though, the automobile was little more than a bright idea being imagined and reimagined by mechanically minded men trying to find efficient ways to travel in carriages without horses. Women were still enjoying the new freedoms made possible by the bicycle,

The author sits behind the wheel of a 35-horsepower, 1916 Dodge touring car at the Auburn Cord Duesenberg Automobile Museum in Indiana; no photos of her 1964 Ford Falcon survive.

ᴄᴄ With your eyes on the road and muscle and brain delicately co-operating with the machine, a woman may ride to new horizons and fill the spaces of her soul with new life and health." —Joan Newton Cuneo in "Out-Door Women," *Good Housekeeping*, June 1910

which grew to enormous popularity in the 1890s. Physical fitness, functional clothing, and unsupervised social outings were just some of the benefits women reaped once they embraced the two-wheeler. But the bicycle revolution ended when the age of the motor car began, and women suddenly found themselves less welcome behind this new form of "wheel." Having explored how women "rode the bicycle to freedom" in my book *Wheels of Change*, I wanted to examine what happened next, when the automobile took over.

I found that like the early motor car itself, women's history with this new technology was full of stops and starts, stalling unexpectedly at times but eventually moving forward. Some women went all in, driving across the country for personal satisfaction or political causes or competing in races to experience the pure thrill of power and speed. Others were more hesitant, cowed by the men who labeled female "automobilists" unfeminine or deterred by the expense or the mechanical breakdowns or the dirt and dust that assaulted those riding in open cars. But enough women pursued the adventures and practical benefits of the automobile that they wrote themselves into the story of its development. That story is chock-full of grit and gumption. So fasten your seat belt. It's going to be a bumpy ride.

CHAPTER 1

America, Meet the Motor Car

In 1910 a woman looks right at home in a race car built by the Croxton-Keeton Motor Company of Massillon, Ohio.

❝ I do not believe the wildest dreamer of us all has for an infinitesimal fraction of a second begun to appreciate what the modern motor car is to do for the twentieth century civilization.”
—"The Prophet of Motoring," *Motor*, April 1904

In 1895 Chicago newspaper publisher Herman H. Kohlsaat had an idea that was as crazy as it was inspired. He decided to hold a race for motor cars. Kohlsaat was intrigued by reports that some 300 Americans were tinkering away on motorized vehicles in their barns and workshops. He knew that European inventors had made great advances in building them and that a newspaper in France had sponsored a well-attended motor-car race there the previous year. "The United States is in the rear of the procession in this branch of inventive progress," Kohlsaat's *Times-Herald* declared on July 9, 1895, "while it should be in the front rank." Toward that end, the paper announced that "Five thousand dollars is hereby offered by the *Times-Herald* for the successful competitors in a horseless carriage or vehicle motor race between Milwaukee and Chicago."

Herman H. Kohlsaat, publisher of the *Chicago Times-Herald*

Background: The front page of Kohlsaat's newspaper announcing the "Prize for Motors" on July 9, 1985

Over the next several weeks, more details of the race emerged. All competing vehicles were required to have at least three wheels, thus ruling out motorized bicycles. They could be propelled by gasoline, electricity, or steam. They had to be large enough to carry a driver and one other person, have at least three lamps for nighttime driving, and include a trumpet, foghorn, or other device to warn people and horses of their approach. Each driver would be accompanied by an umpire to monitor his progress. Cash prizes would be awarded to the first car to finish, as well as to other competitors based on their race performance and the results of a battery of scientific tests on their vehicles.

Kohlsaat scheduled the race for November 2, which he thought would be late enough to allow contestants to finish their vehicles, but early enough to avoid Chicago's unpredictable, late autumn weather. Alas, the publisher underestimated how much time the inventors needed. Although the September 28 edition of the *Times-Herald* reported that 83 vehicles had entered the race, only two were ready by the deadline. Oscar Mueller, son of a plumbing goods manufacturer from

Decatur, Illinois, arrived with a gasoline-powered vehicle that his father had imported from inventor Karl Benz of Germany. J. Frank Duryea and his brother Charles, who in 1893 had built and road tested the first gasoline-powered motor car in the United States, brought their latest model. Kohlsaat pitted Mueller against the Duryea brothers in an exhibition on November 2 and pushed back the main event to Thanksgiving Day, November 28. Mueller won the November 2 exhibition and the $500 prize.

In 1886 Karl Benz of Germany received the patent for his three-wheeled, 2/3-horsepower, gasoline-fueled Benz Patent-Motorwagen, widely considered the first automobile. His wife, Bertha, financed the development of the vehicle and took her teenage sons on its first long-distance drive, a round-trip of about 130 miles to visit her mother.

While the weather for the November 2 exhibition had been perfect, conditions for the November 28 race were perfectly awful. Twelve inches of wet, heavy snow had fallen on Chicago two days earlier, and a subsequent warm-up left the road thick with slush and mud. Fortunately, officials had shortened the course soon after the contest was pushed to late November. Drivers would now race from Jackson Park in Chicago to the neighboring town of Evanston and back again, a total of just over 54 miles. Though the *Times-Herald* listed 31 entries for the race in its November 27 edition, only 6 lined up for the start the following day. All of the drivers were men. Oscar Mueller and Frank Duryea were there, along with gasoline-powered vehicles sponsored by two New York businesses, the De La Vergne Refrigerating Machine Company and the department store R.H. Macy and Company. Two electric carmakers, the Sturges Electric Motocycle Company of Chicago and Morris and Salom of Philadelphia, also had entries.

Starting times were staggered, with Duryea going out first at 8:55 a.m. He covered the initial eight miles of the course in one hour, but soon afterward his left front tire struck a deep rut in the road, causing the vehicle's steering arm to break off. Drivers were barred from getting outside help on the course, but Duryea stretched the rules by borrowing tools from a nearby blacksmith shop and fixing the car himself. By that time the De La Vergne car was out of the race, succumbing

Above: Artist Robert Schulz commemorated the 1895 *Times-Herald* race in this painting several decades after the fact.

Right: J. Frank Duryea (left) sits with his umpire, Arthur W. White of Toronto, Canada, in the car Duryea drove in the race.

to the icy roads and snowdrifts after only three miles. The drivers of the two electric cars also called it quits before the halfway point, acknowledging the limited range of their batteries but satisfied that they had demonstrated their cars' abilities to perform under challenging conditions.

Duryea reached Evanston in third place, behind Mueller and the Macy car, but his opponents suffered setbacks on the homestretch. The Macy car lost close to an hour and a half for repairs after hitting a horse-drawn carriage whose driver refused to yield. The car's motor finally gave out at 6:20 p.m. Meanwhile, Mueller had to stop several times to fix a damaged clutch and wrap twine around his tires to keep them from spinning on the slick roads. The continued effort took its toll. About five miles from the finish, Mueller

Reprinted from the *Horseless Age* weekly magazine

NEW YORK, NY • APRIL 26, 1899

"HORSEY" HORSELESS CARRIAGES

Uriah Smith, of Battle Creek, Mich., believes that the greatest impediment to the general use of motor vehicles is the fact that some horses, particularly those in the country, are frightened by them.

To obviate this danger he had devised the form of carriage shown in the illustration, having the front portion terminating in the shape of a horse's head and neck. This expedient, he thinks, would allay the fears of any equine, for to the head on approach "it would have all the appearance of a horse and carriage, and hence raise no fears in any skittish animal; for the live horse would be thinking of another horse, and before he could discover his error and see that he had been fooled, the strange carriage would be passed, and then it would be too late to grow frantic and fractious."

The inventor also recommends this device as a wind break and as a receptacle for gasolene [*sic*].

lost consciousness from exhaustion, and his umpire had to drive the car back to Jackson Park. When they arrived at 8:53 p.m., Duryea was waiting for them. He had finished the course at 7:18 p.m. after 10 hours and 23 minutes on the road, including 1 hour and 35 minutes for repairs. Officials awarded $2,000 to Duryea; $1,500 to Mueller; $500 to the Macy car; and $500 to the Sturges Electric. They split the remaining $500 among vehicles that

> **To my mind, the horse is doomed. The horseless vehicle is the coming wonder ... It is only a question of time when the carriages and trucks in every large city will be run with motors."** —Thomas Edison, *New York World*, 1895

performed well on the scientific tests, including some that had not taken part in the race.

In the end, Duryea's ability to persevere despite the messy weather was a boon for the motor car. Several newspapers took the opportunity to declare the downfall of the horse, echoing comments inventor Thomas Edison had made a few weeks earlier in the *New York World*. In its race recap, the *Advocate* of Topeka, Kansas, considered the benefits of this new form of transportation. "For private use, as compared with the horse carriage, it has many points in its favor," the newspaper reported. "The space required for stabling would be merely that occupied by its own bulk; and its running expenses would be limited to the fuel consumed and such repairs as might occasionally be required."

Frank and Charles Duryea were quick to capitalize on their success in the *Times-Herald* race. Their Duryea Motor Wagon Company sold its first vehicle in February 1896 and built a dozen more cars that year, making it the largest automobile manufacturer in the United States. But the brothers fought over recognition and control and ended their partnership before the twentieth century began. Fortunately, there were plenty of other industrious men to pick up the slack. By the end of 1899, over 30 new companies had started producing automobiles. In 1900 that figure more than doubled, and American automobile manufacturers turned out a total of 1,681 steam-, 1,575 electric-, and 936 gasoline-powered vehicles.

People spent a lot of time in the early 1900s discussing the relative merits of these three power sources. In 1904 *Motor* magazine invited prominent manufacturers of each type of vehicle to list its benefits for the publication. Elmer Apperson, whose promising Haynes-Apperson car missed out on the *Times-Herald* race because it got into an accident on the way to the starting line, represented gasoline-powered vehicles. Apperson wrote that the fuel for gasoline engines was available "in every town and at every cross-roads store." He pointed out that, unlike steam, gasoline would not freeze in cold weather. And gasoline engines were noiseless. What's more, gasoline-powered vehicles could run as far as 1,000 miles before the engine needed service. By comparison, Apperson noted, steam engines could only run 100 miles, and electrics averaged 30 to 40 miles on a single charge. He added that gasoline vehicles were more pleasant to drive, with no steam gauges or battery indicators to monitor.

Windsor T. White, who manufactured the White Steamer with his brothers Rollin and Walter, argued the case for steam-powered vehicles. White wrote that steam engines had practically no vibrations or noise while in use, making them superior to the other options. He added that, unlike driving a gasoline-powered vehicle, driving a steamer did not require changing gears or using a clutch. Steamers also were flexible, able to proceed at slow or fast speeds with equal ease. And most Americans understood how steam engines worked (because steam was used to power locomotives and other machines), while few people understood how internal combustion engines worked in gasoline-powered cars. Because of that, White said people in steamers would have less trouble finding help with emergency roadside repairs.

Walter C. Baker of Baker Electrics wrote the column on the benefits of electric vehicles. Baker, who counted Thomas Edison among his customers, listed several reasons why electrics were particularly appropriate for female drivers. First, since electric cars required no steam, oil, or other messy fuel, women didn't need protective clothing as they would in gasoline and steam vehicles.

❝ If women in general understood the vast pleasure to be derived from driving their own car I feel confident that the number of women motorists soon would be vastly increased. There is a wonderful difference between sitting calmly by while another is driving and actually handling a car by herself."
—Mrs. A. Sherman Hitchcock, *Motor*, April 1904

Detail of a 1913 ad for Baker Electrics cars. As roads improved and Americans took longer car trips, electrics became impractical, all but disappearing by 1935. But rising gas prices in the 1970s and antipollution laws in the 1990s would bring renewed interest in electrics, making them and gas-electric hybrids a viable option in the twenty-first century.

Furthermore, electrics were "strong, durable, attractive, light, refined, and safe for a gentleman or lady, and we may say for even a child to drive." Like Apperson and White, Baker claimed his cars were quiet, and he also pointed out they were odorless and vibration-free. He said the battery, which gave the electric its power, did require regular attention but "the minimum of care returns a maximum of results." Baker also addressed the driving speed of electrics, which tended to be slower than that of gasoline-powered vehicles. The electric's speed, he wrote, was "greater than that of a horse."

Electrics and steamers jockeyed for the lead as the most popular automobile engine types in the United States until 1903, when Ohio-born Ransom Olds hit the big time. His Olds Motor Works set out to develop a practical gas-powered vehicle for the American

public that was light and sturdy, markedly different from the heavy touring cars popular in Europe. Olds spent more than a year producing 11 prototypes, only to have a gasoline fire in his factory destroy 10 of them. The remaining model, a small car with a curved dash, resembled a sled on wheels. Olds had an employee drive that model from his headquarters in Detroit to the 1901 automobile show in New York City, where a dealer was so impressed that he ordered 1,000 cars. Production grew to 4,000 in 1903, accounting for 36 percent of all American-made motor cars that year and leading gasoline-powered vehicles to dominate steamers and electrics for the first time. Priced at $650—a speedometer and buggy-style top were extra—the Olds Curved Dash was the first low-priced, mass-produced automobile in the United States.

Ransom Olds was the first auto manufacturer to use an assembly line, an arrangement in which the work in progress passes from one person to the next until it is complete. But Michigan native Henry Ford took it to a whole new level, introducing mechanical conveyor belts to move the work down the assembly line. Ford had been tinkering with motor cars since the 1890s, attracting investors who backed him in a series of businesses culminating in the Ford Motor Company in 1903. He emphasized the importance of uniformity in the cars he produced. In his autobiography he noted, "We build our cars absolutely interchangeable. All parts are as nearly alike as chemical analysis, the finest machinery, and the finest workmanship can make them." Over the next two decades Ford turned out a series of "alphabet models"—Model A, B, and the popular Model N—that made the company the top producer of automobiles in the United States every year from 1906 through 1926.

Left: Henry Ford takes a spin in his first car, the Ford Quadricycle, in 1896.

Background: An early twentieth-century gas station at the corner of Texas and Atlantic Avenues in Atlantic City, New Jersey

'Weird and Impossible Names'

In the 1890s one of the most animated topics of discussion regarding the motor car involved what to call it. While the *Chicago Times-Herald* was planning its horseless carriage race in 1895, the paper invited readers to offer names for this new vehicle. The editors awarded $500 to the man who suggested their favorite term: Motocycle. But that didn't put the issue to rest. "The question of a name for the automobile vehicles is still agitating many worthy persons," reported *Scientific American* in 1899, "and the result has been a collection of weird and impossible names which are amusing to say the least." Among those listed in the magazine were Electro-mobile (referring to the electric car), Locomotive (referring to the steam car), Auto-carriage, Kinetic, Propellor, Self-motor, Autogo, Autocam, and Autopher. The latter includes the last six letters of St. Christopher, considered by many to be the patron saint of travelers.

One term that did not curry much favor was Automobile. In an 1899 issue of the *Horseless Age* magazine, a writer rejected that term because it was coined in France. He expected it would "largely be weeded out from our common speech because of its length and foreign parentage." He preferred Motor Vehicle.

A family enjoys a drive in their Model T touring car, circa 1915.

Henry Ford assessed the marketplace in a 1906 letter to *Automobile* magazine. "The greatest need to-day is a light, low-priced car with an up-to-date engine of ample horse-power, and built of the very best material," he wrote. "It must be powerful enough for American roads and capable of carrying its passengers anywhere that a horse-drawn vehicle will go." Ford succeeded in producing the vehicle he described when the company introduced the Model T in October 1908. Nicknamed the "Flivver" or "Tin Lizzie," the Model T sold for $825 in 1908, but thanks to advances in mass production, the price fell steadily over the years to a low of $260 in 1925. Ford called the Model T the "universal car," and it nearly was. Although earlier, more expensive motor cars were bought mainly by wealthy people, the Model T made automobile travel available to the middle class, and they

Lillian Sheridan

On January 21, 1922, a young woman from Seattle, Washington, sent an admiring letter to Henry Ford. "I am like a school-girl movie fan with you," Lillian Sheridan wrote, requesting a letter or a signed photograph in return. Despite the affection she expressed for Ford, however, this was not a piece of fan mail. Sheridan was a crack sales-woman of Ford automobiles and had recently become a sales manager with an all-female sales force. She was writing to tell Ford about what the *Seattle Post-Intelligencer* called, "the first exclusively women's Ford sales organization on record, as far as is known here."

Sheridan started out selling only tires in 1917, but quickly worked her way up to the whole vehicle. "I just love selling Fords," she told the *Seattle Daily Times*. "I have always wanted to be able to handle a commodity of wide popular demand. Even while selling tires I often thought that it must be wonderful to handle big motor cars and earn the big commissions they pay." Sheridan inter-viewed more than 40 female applicants before selecting the 5 who would join her sales team. She gained such local fame that a flower grower named his new, crowd-pleasing, orange-and-white dahlia "The Lillian Sheridan."

Sheridan married Lieutenant Herbert Phillips of the Washington National Guard in 1924, and then teamed up with him to sell cars. "Mr. Phillips talks speed and power and I speak of beauty and design," she told the *Seattle Daily Times*. Alas, her commitment to Henry Ford did not survive the marriage. Lieutenant and Mrs. Phillips sold Chevrolets.

Reprinted from the *Motor Way* monthly magazine

CHICAGO, IL · JULY 1907

WOMAN GIVES OLD KNOX SEVERE TEST

A run that was a record in several respects was made June 2, when two women drove a 1903 car alone from Springfield to New York in 12 hours total time and less than 10 hours actual running time. The distance is 157 miles, or more than the average day's run in the Glidden contest and more than was the daily task of the cars in the sealed bonnet contest of the Automobile Club of America.

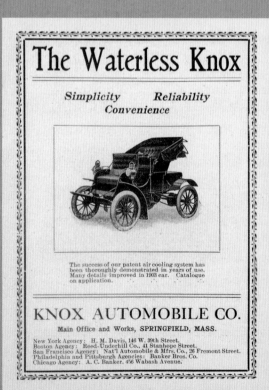

The Waterless Knox

Simplicity   Reliability
Convenience

The success of our patent air cooling system has been thoroughly demonstrated in years of use. Many details improved in 1903 car. Catalogue on application.

KNOX AUTOMOBILE CO.
Main Office and Works, SPRINGFIELD, MASS.

New York Agency: H. M. Davis, 146 W. 39th Street.
Boston Agency: Reed-Underhill Co., 41 Stanhope Street.
San Francisco Agency: Nat'l Automobile & Mfrs. Co., 26 Fremont Street.
Philadelphia and Pittsburgh Agencies: Banker Bros. Co.
Chicago Agency: A. C. Banker, 456 Wabash Avenue.

The women were Mrs. E. Philips, wife of Dr. Calvin Philips, and Mrs. Arthur Jervis, both of New York. The car was a single cylinder Knox of ten horsepower that has been in continuous service since 1903. The car is that of Mrs. Philips, and she was the driver. Mrs. Philips is as proficient in the care of the car and even in its repair as a professional chauffeur, and takes pride in going out alone with it. The start from Springfield was made at 10 a.m. The roads were very bad, especially from Springfield to Hartford, but the women brought the car through without mishap, stopping for meals more than two hours and arriving at the Rutland, 57th street and Broadway, at 10 p.m.

Note: The Glidden contest was an endurance road rally for automobiles started in 1902. Also, the Springfield referred to here is in Massachusetts.

Above: Ford Model Ts come off the assembly line in this 1913 photo.

Right: Clara Bryant Ford, wife of Henry, drives a Model N with Myrle Clarkson, a Ford company telephone operator, in 1906.

embraced it in record numbers. Output grew every year, until in 1923–1924, two-thirds of all the automobiles registered in the United States were Model Ts. By the time the last Model T rolled off the assembly line in 1927, Ford had produced just over 15 million of them.

Ford couldn't have achieved its success without marketing cars to women as well as men. In both 1911 and 1915, the company issued special booklets aimed at female consumers. But like many in the early automobile industry, Henry Ford had mixed feelings about women's emancipation in the new century and, in particular, their place on the nation's roads. While his wife Clara posed for publicity photos driving Ford automobiles, Henry bypassed his revolutionary, gasoline-powered Model T when he chose a new vehicle for her in 1908. Instead, he bought Clara a more sedate, less adventurous electric car. ⚙

MOTORING LAWS

As the motor car became popular in the United States, the need quickly arose for laws to regulate speed and safety. Here are some of the more unusual laws and practices from the dawn of the automobile age.

PENNA 1906
11907

LICENSE PLATES Shortly after the turn of the century local officials started to require motor vehicles to display tags that identified them. In 1901 New York became the first state to register cars and directed all owners to make their own license plates showing their initials. In 1903 Massachusetts became the first state to issue license plates, choosing numbers over letters. Three years later Pennsylvania set a new precedent by issuing plates that had to be replaced every year. Every state in the Union required license plates on motor cars by 1918.

❯ ADVANCED WARNING

In 1894 Vermont passed a law dictating that "a person of mature age" must run at least one-eighth of a mile ahead of any steam-powered vehicle to warn people traveling with horses or other animals that could be frightened. At night the runner was required to carry a red light. This and similar laws passed in Michigan and New York were originally meant to regulate steam-powered farm machinery, but they were applied to steam-powered automobiles as well.

❯ LIABILITY

In 1901 a court in New York City ruled that the passengers in cars that broke the speed limit should be assessed the same fine or other punishment as the driver.

❯ SPEEDING

In 1902 several cities in Illinois took extreme measures to stop speeders. The mayor of Glencoe stationed police officers with stopwatches at points along a designated roadway to compute the time it took drivers to cover the distance. If a driver went too fast, the officers tightened a wire rope across the road to stop the automobile and arrest the offender. Another mayor dispensed with the wire and had his officers throw logs in front of speeding vehicles!

❯ DRIVING HOURS

In 1905 the following ordinance was upheld on appeal in Marin County, California: "No person shall run an automobile on any of the ... highways of Marin County between the hours of sunset of any day and of sunrise on the day following." Violators were to be fined or imprisoned.

❯ REGISTRATION

Before 1907, motorists in Missouri were required to register their vehicles in every county in which they planned to drive. The registration fees to drive legally in all of Missouri's counties totaled $295.50 in 1906. The following year, county fees were replaced by one $5 state registration fee.

Left: Two police officers use an umbrella topped with "Stop" and "Go" signs to regulate traffic in the District of Columbia in 1913.

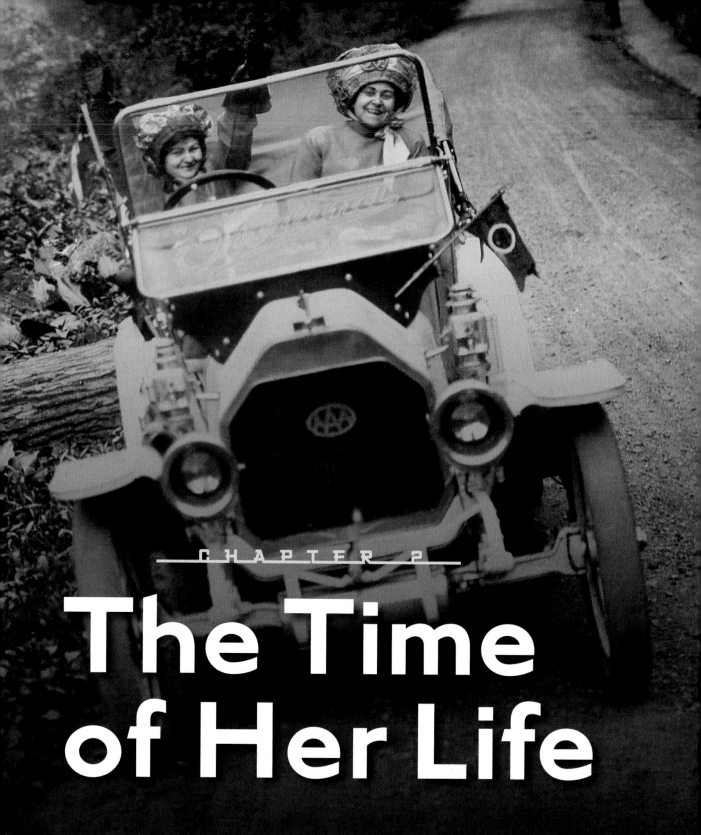

CHAPTER 2

The Time of Her Life

Blanche Stuart Scott of Rochester, New York, and her passenger are all smiles during a photo break on their 1910 drive across the United States. For more on Scott, see page 50.

" [Women], as a whole, are utterly unfitted to pilot ships, command armies, or operate automobiles, and through no fault of their own. They were born that way." — S.P. Foster, *Motor*, May 1914

Montgomery Rollins was absolutely certain that because women didn't play baseball, they had no business behind the wheel of a motor car. Rollins, a New England banker who considered himself an expert on safe and sane driving, explained his thinking in a 1909 article in the *Outlook*, a leading weekly magazine. Women, he wrote, were "not trained to think of two things at once," a skill he felt was of the greatest importance when driving. By comparison, he declared, a man "is trained from earliest youth in playing baseball, where he has to watch two or three bases at once, he is trained in a thousand and one ways to act quickly." Rollins was not alone in his assessment that driving was a masculine activity. His was just one of several arguments that aimed to keep female motorists off the road at the dawn of the automobile age.

Objections to women driving centered around three main themes. Like Rollins, some critics believed women did not possess the skill, intelligence, or temperament to be good motorists. Others were concerned that driving would somehow undermine women's femininity, exposing them to the grit and grime of the road and causing them to develop unladylike physical strength. Still others feared that the sense of independence women gained from operating motor cars might upset the social order, blurring the lines between male and female roles. These worries colored much of the conversation about women and cars during the first two decades of the twentieth century,

"Woman was not created to exert great physical strength nor to stand even comparatively light strains over a long period of time," wrote Jennie Davis, in the May 1914 issue of *Motor* magazine. Two months earlier, the magazine had asked its audience to answer the question, "Do Women Make Good Drivers?" *Motor* presented responses from four readers, with Davis voicing "A Woman's View." While she felt that taking an

Men look on in dismay as a woman lifts heavy weights without breaking a sweat in this 1880s cartoon by Frederick B. Opper titled "The Development of the 'Weaker Sex' (and the Demoralization of the Dude)."

occasional drive in the country could be "a delight and a benefit" for most women, Davis cautioned them to avoid traffic. "Driving in severe traffic conditions is so great a strain that no ordinary woman should attempt it," she wrote. Davis explained that through their experiences in the world at large, men had developed quick instincts that would help them to react appropriately in emergency situations. She felt most women did not have that training, so instead of acting instinctively, they were likely to reason things out. That would not serve them well with an out-of-control car careening toward them.

Just over a year after Davis expressed her views, Magistrate Frederick B. House of New York City's West Farms Court declared all women unfit to drive in his ruling in the case of Lillian M. Siddens. On August 31, 1915, Siddens had the regrettable experience of running down a Bronx patrolman with her car. Fortunately, the patrolman was not seriously injured. The magistrate fined Siddens $50 for reckless driving, which she promptly paid, but before she was dismissed, House had some parting words. "In my opinion," he told her, "no woman should be allowed to operate an automobile.

Millionaire businesswoman Madam C.J. Walker takes friends for a spin in 1911.

Reprinted from the *Chicago Defender* weekly newspaper

CHICAGO, IL · AUGUST 10, 1912

THE FAIR SEX AT THE WHEEL

Geniuses are born every hour and know no sex. We men occasionally wonder at women of other races driving automobiles. We must now stop to admire the grit of our own these days. A party of five were whirled up Fifth avenue [*sic*] in Mr. Whitaker's car, driven by Mme. Ernestine I. Jackson, who displayed no nervousness, in fact, I don't believe she is afraid of a mouse, and we were safely landed at our homes, and the "smoke went up the chimney just the same." Among other well-known ladies who are capable drivers are Mrs. H.J. Branson, Mrs. C.L. Reese, Mrs. William Felton and Mrs. Walter McClennon. —Ex.

Note: The *Chicago Defender* focuses on the African-American community.

Above: A female driver gets stuck on a muddy road during an endurance race in 1907.

Right: This Cadillac ad from 1912 introduces the first crankless car.

The C A R
THAT HAS NO CRANK

In the first place, she hasn't the strength, and, in the second place, she is very apt to lose her head."

Even those who encouraged women to take the wheel admitted that they had to come to terms with their insecurities. Mrs. A. Sherman Hitchcock, who frequently wrote magazine articles urging her gender to embrace the motor car, acknowledged, "Nine out of ten women who are asked why they don't drive their own cars, invariably answer in the same way—that they are too nervous." Hitchcock agreed those who were overwhelmed by nerves should avoid driving, but cautioned, "the trouble of nervousness is greatly exaggerated by many women, and would undoubtedly in most cases wear away rapidly as confidence in herself became established."

Concerns that handling an automobile would threaten a woman's femininity were grounded in the fact that early motoring was a sweaty, messy business, especially when the car in question was powered by gasoline. Until Cadillac introduced the electric self-starter in 1912, a motorist had to position herself in front of her vehicle and vigorously turn a hand crank to start a gasoline engine. If the car stalled during the ride, she would have to get out and crank it again. Since roads were not always paved, she often undertook this effort surrounded by clouds of dust, or if it had rained, mounds of mud. Punctured tires also were common on unpaved roads, requiring drivers to muscle through a tire change or hope for a passing motorist to stop or send help. These scenarios were not at all consistent with the view of women as dainty

A female motorist turns a crank to start her car on a dirt road in 1914. It was not until 1920 that most cars had self-starters instead of hand cranks.

and delicate, but early female motorists repeatedly proved they were up to the task. Sometimes they even garnered praise from men. In a 1905 article on the "tire question," a mechanical engineer named Roger C. Aldrich proudly reported, "My wife, who is not above the average woman in strength, can put on a tire as easily and well as I."

Many of the men who worried that driving would foster independence in women were also thinking about their own role in American society. The United States had changed a great deal in the 1800s, evolving from a country of family farms to one in which the majority of middle-class men worked in offices or factories. Instead of being at home all day to pass down skills and values to their children, these men had to cede a lot of that responsibility to their wives. The home became the woman's sphere, while the workplace and much of the outside world became the man's. But several factors at the turn of the century

Competitive driver Joan Newton Cuneo changes a tire on her 1908 Rainier automobile. Cuneo's car was equipped with Fisk bolted-on tires with removable rims, a relatively new invention. Instead of removing the whole tire frame, Cuneo could replace the punctured rim with a new one that was properly inflated (seen here) in only five minutes.

seemed to threaten this dichotomy, as women started attending college, entering the workforce, and fighting to win the vote. The automobile provided yet another means for women to break free from the bonds that kept them at home. "Learning to handle the car has wrought my emancipation, my freedom," wrote wife and mother Christine McGaffey Frederick in 1912. "The auto permits the commuter's wife still to be a social being. She need not be isolated or marooned."

Mrs. A. Sherman Hitchcock called out the men who didn't want their wives driving the family car in a 1913 article in *American Homes and Gardens*. "His real reason," she wrote, "is without doubt in most cases a wholly selfish one—he fears her proficiency and doesn't want her to use the car as often as she would wish." Indeed, at the start of the twentieth century, many wealthy men followed Henry Ford's lead by keeping their powerful gasoline automobiles for themselves and buying their wives electric cars. Manufacturers used the electrics' limited range and lower average speed as part of a sales pitch to capture the female market. In 1908 the Babcock Electric Carriage Company declared its vehicle perfect "For Wife or Daughter, Mother or Sister."

Reprinted from the *Automobile* weekly magazine

NEW YORK, NY • JUNE 6, 1903

ALICE ROOSEVELT BECOMES A MOTORIST.

WASHINGTON, D.C., May 30—The use of the automobile is becoming almost universal among the official and social set of Washington. The latest recruit is Miss Alice Roosevelt, eldest daughter of the President of the United States, who has just purchased a $2,500 United States Long Distance touring car. Frequently of late Miss Roosevelt has been seen riding in the automobile of Countess Cassini, niece of the Russian Ambassador, and it was freely predicted that she would have a car of her own before the summer was over. The machine arrived in Washington during the present week, and was used by its fair owner for the first time this morning to convey her to the railroad station.

The first ride was rather exciting. Coming down Pennsylvania Avenue, Miss Roosevelt found herself in the midst of a number of fire engines and trucks, which were responding to an alarm of fire. Handling the machine like a veteran, she skilfully [*sic*] guided the vehicle through the maze of fire apparatus, and displayed much coolness in a rather trying position, proving that she is competent to drive an automobile.

No. 743,801.   PATENTED NOV. 10, 1903.

M. ANDERSON.
WINDOW CLEANING DEVICE.
APPLICATION FILED JUNE 18, 1903.

• MOTOR GIRL •

NO MODEL.

Fig. 2.

Mary Anderson

36

Though thousands of innovative men had a hand in developing the motor car, it took a woman to figure out the best way for drivers to see in stormy weather. When Mary Anderson visited New York City in 1903, she was surprised to learn that electric trolley car operators had no easy way of clearing snow, sleet, or rain from their windshields. Some tried to wipe the mess away with horsehair brushes as they drove. Others opened the windshields, which were split horizontally, and traveled with the elements hitting them and their passengers instead of the glass. Anderson started sketching a more practical solution (background) while she was still in New York. Back in her native Alabama, she assembled a prototype and filed for a patent.

Anderson's "Window-Cleaning Device" received a 17-year patent from the U.S. government on November 10, 1903. It included a "radially-swinging arm" made of wood and rubber that was mounted above the outer windshield and was operated by a handle inside the vehicle. The initial response was not positive. Critics feared drivers would be distracted by the wiper's movement or find it difficult to manipulate the handle while also holding the steering wheel and shifting gears. Anderson never went into production with her device, but within a decade similar windshield wipers would become standard issue on most automobiles.

Anderson was not an inventor by trade. In fact, this was her only patent. She spent most of her life managing an apartment building in Birmingham, Alabama, that she owned with her sister and mother. She died at age 87 on June 27, 1953.

Fig. 1.

Witnesses
Milton Lenoir.
Watts T. Estabrook

Fig. 5.

Inventor
Mary Anderson

by
her Attorney

Above: In 1912 a young woman uses a hand-cranked battery charger to power up her Columbia Mark 68 Victoria electric car. One impediment to the early popularity of electric vehicles was the fact that in 1912 only about 16 percent of American homes were wired for electricity.

Right: This 1908 ad touts the Babcock Electric as the perfect car for women—and children—who want to drive. It was not until 1909 that the first state—Pennsylvania—placed an age limit on driving, issuing licenses only to people 18 and older.

FOR WIFE OR DAUGHTER
MOTHER OR SISTER

What More Acceptable Gift Than A

Babcock Electric

The Automobile That Women and Children Can Operate With Ease and Safety.

Adapted for any Kind of Service in City or Suburbs.

MODEL 6, VICTORIA, PRICE $1,700.

"When You Build Right, IT IS Right and Works Right."—Babcock

Five Models   *Send for Catalogue*

BABCOCK ELECTRIC CARRIAGE CO., Builders

New York Branch, 1591 Broadway, Cor. 48th St.   **224 West Utica St., Buffalo, N.Y.**

In 1911 the Anderson Electric Car Company urged men to buy its Detroit Electric model "for your bride-to-be—or your bride of many Junes ago," promising it would be "the most considerate choice for her permanent happiness, comfort, luxury, safety."

Despite these efforts, some women were as smitten as men with the gasoline car. In 1909 a family friend of poet Minna Irving suggested that she get an electric, but she had other ideas. "The smell of gasolene [*sic*] is to me as battle smoke to the soldier, and salt sea air to the sailor," she wrote, "and so I decided against the electric." Over the next five years, improvements in gasoline vehicles, such as the electric self-starter and the electric gear shift—which replaced the cumbersome gear shift lever with a series of buttons—made them even more popular with women. "Dealers handling gasoline cars in the last few seasons have found it more and more to their profit to devote increasing attention to women," declared the *Tennessean* in 1914. The newspaper noted that women weren't only coming in to purchase their own cars; they also seemed to be "casting the deciding vote" as to which car their husbands should buy.

Advocates for female drivers urged them to learn as much about their cars as possible. The Automobile School of the West Side Young Men's Christian Association in New York City started admitting women as pupils in 1915, and two staff members included a chapter titled "Women as Drivers" in their 1918 book, *Putnam's Automobile Handbook*. "So far as mastering the mechanical and technical details of a car, women seem to be just as apt as most men, if they take it seriously enough," authors H. Clifford Brokaw and Charles A. Starr observed. They noted that female students readily embraced the task of taking a car apart bolt by bolt and then putting it back together again. In fact, the authors felt their female students exhibited the same enthusiasm when they worked their way up to driving through New York City's busiest intersection, Fifth Avenue and 42nd Street. "The women always enjoy that," they reported, proving that not all women withered in traffic. Each one, they wrote, "shows she is having the time of her life."

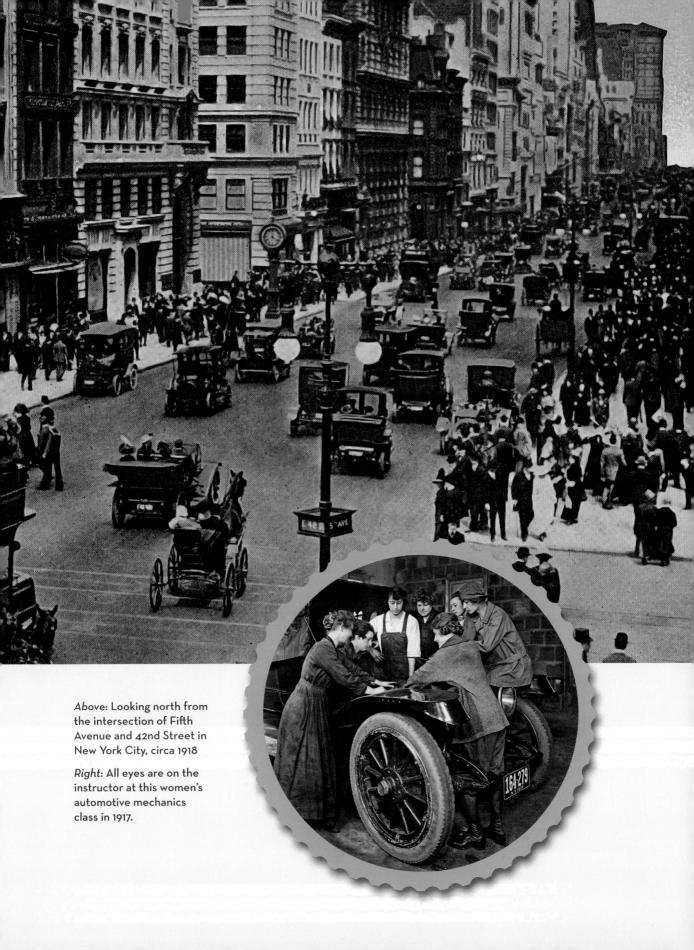

Above: Looking north from the intersection of Fifth Avenue and 42nd Street in New York City, circa 1918

Right: All eyes are on the instructor at this women's automotive mechanics class in 1917.

MIND YOUR MANNERS

Maybe it was the speed. Or the power. Or the
opportunity to flaunt their shiny new automobiles.
Whatever the reason, sometimes drivers could be
just plain rude, and by the early 1900s, etiquette
experts began to notice. So they started dispensing
advice like that found here, taken from books of the day.

> **DON'T STARE:** "Do not stare at another's car, nor, if at a standstill, examine the mechanism. This is the height of rudeness."
—*Everyday Etiquette*, 1905

> **DON'T SHOW OFF:** "When passing an auto of inferior horsepower, do not choose that moment to exhibit your own greater speed. Be careful also not to give such a car your dust nor (so far as you can avoid) to sicken its occupants with the smell of your motor's gasolene."
—*Everyday Etiquette*, 1905

> **ACT RESPONSIBLY:** "A person who should run over or into another without stopping to inquire about the victim, and to offer assistance, could not expect to be considered a gentleman. Such ruffianly conduct is unfortunately not uncommon."
—*Manners and Social Usages*, 1907

> **CHECK WITH YOUR PASSENGERS:** "A considerate driver never starts his car until his companions declare themselves comfortable and prepared to progress."—*Encyclopædia of Etiquette*, 1912

> **BE A GOOD HOST:** "The host or hostess of a motor-car who invites a friend or two for a day's or afternoon's run should provide the necessary refreshments, or, stopping at a roadside inn for tea, pay the cost of the beverages and food ordered. This is the rule, unless other arrangements by mutual consent have been arrived at."
—*Putnam's Handbook of Etiquette*, 1913

> **SHOW RESPECT:** "When three ladies enter a motor-car or carriage the young unmarried lady should take the back seat and the two married ladies should occupy the front seat; this is a matter of courtesy on the part of a young lady due to married ladies and not strictly demanded by etiquette."
—*Manners and Rules of Good Society*, 1913

Two couples stop for a picnic in this 1907 poster advertising cars produced by the Daimler Motors Corporation of Germany.

CHAPTER 3

Going the Distance

Alice Ramsey was only 22 years old in 1909 when she became the first woman to drive an automobile across the United States (above). She later wrote that she was "born mechanical," a trait she believed she inherited from her father.

"She was finding the one secret of long-distance driving—namely, driving; keeping on, thinking by fifty-mile units, not by ten-mile stretches ... and not fretting over anything whatever ... Nothing, it seemed, could halt her level flight across the giant land." —Sinclair Lewis, describing Claire Boltwood in his novel *Free Air*, 1919

It was pouring rain in New York City on June 9, 1909, and Alice Ramsey said she and her three companions looked like "a quartet of nuns." They wore identical rubber helmets on their heads, rubber capes on their shoulders, and rubber ponchos that reached down to their shoes. But as the women took their places in their brand-new, 30-horsepower Maxwell DA touring car, what concerned them most wasn't their rain gear. It was the four bouquets of pink carnations that well-wishers from their hometown had just given them. The well-wishers, members of the Elks fraternal lodge of Hackensack, New Jersey, had assumed bouquets were an appropriate gift for ladies about to embark on a long trip. Though the women appreciated the gesture, there was no place in the overstuffed automobile to store flowers. So they grudgingly placed the dripping buds on their laps.

If the Elks had miscalculated, they were to be forgiven. After all, there was little precedent for the journey the foursome was about to begin. Ramsey hoped to become the first woman to drive across the United States from coast to coast. Her three passengers—her friend, Hermine Jahns, and her sisters-in-law, Nettie Powell and Margaret Atwood—were excited to be along for the ride. The travelers knew the trip would be rough at times, over unpaved and often uncharted roads. But they also knew they had a safety net. The trip was being sponsored by the Maxwell-Briscoe Motor Company. Besides donating the car Ramsey would drive, the company also would pay her expenses, publicize her progress, and provide support at Maxwell dealerships along the way.

Backing the venture was a smart business decision. Ramsey's journey would generate lots of publicity for Maxwell-Briscoe. Her success would solidify the Maxwell's reputation as a safe, durable vehicle and forever link it with a historic achievement. Ramsey had shown impressive skill competing in two long-distance races in the New York area, and

Travelers (left to right) Hermine Jahns, Margaret Atwood, Nettie Powell, and Alice Ramsey pose with bouquets of pink carnations in front of the New York City Maxwell-Briscoe dealership before embarking on their cross-country journey.

the company hoped her confidence and intrepid spirit would inspire more women to drive cars—preferably Maxwells. Still, reaching the West Coast was by no means guaranteed. A year earlier, a cross-country attempt by two Idaho women had ended in failure. Minerva Teape and her daughter, Vera Teape McKelvie, had planned to drive their four-horsepower Waltham automobile from Portland, Maine, to Portland, Oregon. They had to call it quits in Kansas City, Missouri, though, when Teape entered a medical facility to treat a severe cold.

By attempting to drive across the continent, Ramsey was following in the footsteps of Americans before her who traversed the country by horse, stagecoach, train, and even bicycle. Two men had accomplished the first successful crossing in an automobile in 1903, six years before Ramsey's attempt. Horatio Nelson Jackson, a Vermont doctor, was visiting San Francisco when he wagered $50 that he could drive a motor car to the East Coast. He teamed up with a mechanic, Sewall K. Crocker, and purchased a slightly used 20-horsepower Winton for the trip. Jackson and Crocker arrived in New York City after 63 and a half days, having spent $8,000 on food, lodging, parts, repairs, and more than 800 gallons of gasoline. In Idaho they also acquired a dog named Bud, who proved to be a sturdy pioneer in his own right.

Top: This 1909 Maxwell ad shows a 30-horsepower touring car similar to the one Ramsey drove.

Bottom: Horatio Nelson Jackson (driving), Sewall K. Crocker, and Bud on their historic 1903 drive

Above: Alice Ramsey (second from left) and her companions are all smiles as they take a break during their grueling trip.

Right: Ramsey changed an estimated 11 tires on her journey, including this one near Rochelle, Illinois.

Five months before Ramsey and her passengers set out from New York City, the *Automobile* magazine declared that "the driving of an automobile has become a task well within the ability of the average woman." Driving across the country, though, brought a new set of challenges. The rainy weather that marred Ramsey's send-off persisted for 3 days, causing the Maxwell to slide across muddy roads and requiring her to stop over and over to secure the chains on its tires. Once the rain stopped, the travelers had what would be the most productive day of the trip, covering the 198 miles from Buffalo, New York, to Cleveland, Ohio, on brick pavement. They made it to Chicago in 10 days, surviving a hit-and-run accident with only a dented hubcap. But western Illinois and Iowa proved to be far greater trouble. Six consecutive days of heavy thunderstorms flooded the unpaved roads, filling deep holes with water and turning the surface into a sticky mess. "There was only one thing to do," Ramsey would later say, "and that was to go ahead as well as we might and try to get out of it." It took her 14 days to cover the approximately 500 miles across Iowa, including 5 days off for rain delays and repairs to the car.

Nebraska brought better weather, though the roads were so full of craters that the women hired a team of horses to tow them through one particularly bad section. From there it was on to Wyoming, where Ramsey had to maneuver through the many irrigation ditches—some 30 feet deep by 60 feet across—that crossed the road. "I admit I scarcely expected to reach the bottom of one of these ditches in really good condition," she would remember, "and my courage rather failed me on the downward journey." After driving across all of southern Wyoming, the travelers were delayed in Utah when an encounter with a prairie dog hole resulted in a broken front axle. Impatient to finish her journey, Ramsey found a blacksmith to repair the old axle, rather than waiting for Maxwell-Briscoe to ship a new one. From there it was rough going through Nevada, but a rejuvenating stay in Lake Tahoe, on the Nevada-California border, steeled the group for the rest of their trip. They finally

" Automobilists by the score were on hand to greet the first women to cross the continent, and when the plucky driver and her companions made their appearance it was the signal for a great outburst of enthusiasm and welcome." —Unnamed San Francisco newspaper quoted in the *Hackensack Republican*, August 19, 1909

arrived in San Francisco on August 7, tired but triumphant. Their 3,800-mile drive had taken 60 days, including 18 days off for rest and repairs.

Long-distance automobile trips gained in popularity after Ramsey's journey. But the floodgates of cross-country motoring really opened in 1915, when the World War in Europe kept U.S. tourists from crossing the Atlantic. By then motorists could drive the Lincoln Highway, the first roadway across the country, though much of it was still unpaved. As 1915 drew to a close, *Motor* magazine estimated that "no fewer than 6,000 motor cars this year traveled from points east of the Mississippi river to the Pacific coast or visa versa." *Motor* helped encourage drivers by offering a silver medal designed by Louis Tiffany, of New York's Tiffany and Company jewelry store, to the owner of every car that made such a journey. Motorists had to register with the magazine, collect affidavits from city officials at the start and finish, and furnish a list of the major towns they visited. As of *Motor*'s December 1915 issue, 69 car owners had received medals, including five women. The magazine repeated the contest in 1916.

Four cars trek across the United States on the Lincoln Highway in 1915. Dedicated on October 31, 1913, the highway stretched from Times Square in New York City to Lincoln Park in San Francisco, California. The map shows the original route.

While most of these travelers undertook their journeys for the fun of it, others had a more deliberate agenda. Women fighting for the right to vote started using the automobile as early as 1910, when the Illinois Equal Suffrage Association sponsored 15 auto tours. "We took our auto tours through the state to get additions to our ranks," said organizer Catherine Waugh McCulloch. "We gathered names by the thousands all along the route." At that time, there was no federal law giving women the right to vote, but some individual states and territories, especially those in the West, had granted that right to their female citizens. The *Chicago Daily Tribune* praised the Illinois suffragists' direct approach for spreading the word and predicted that the automobile would continue to be an important part of their state campaign. "No doubt we shall

Reprinted from the *Sun* daily newspaper

NEW YORK, NY • OCTOBER 3, 1913

WOMAN WILL DRIVE TAXICAB.

Mrs. Schultz Owns Her Machine and It Will Be for Public Hire.

Mrs. Olive Schultz will be at the beginning of next week New York's first woman driver of a public taxicab. The car is her own five passenger Buick and will be made into a taxicab by installing a meter.

Mrs. Schultz, who is a licensed chauffeuse and was the official scout of Gen. Rosalie Jones's Albany and Washington hikes, has driven her car for hire for some time in answer to phone calls. But now she intends to take up her station for business in front of the Woman's Political Union headquarters, at 13 West Forty-second street. Part of her earnings will be devoted to suffrage.

"I expect to have many calls from women," said Mrs. Schultz yesterday, "as soon as they find how much more careful as drivers women are than men. I expect also to be patronized by theatregoers, and for the night work I shall have a young woman companion. She was a pupil of mine last summer and can run the car in an emergency."

Note: "General" Rosalie Jones was an attorney who led suffragists on long hikes to help publicize their cause.

Olive Schultz

Blanche Stuart Scott

50

Although Alice Ramsey was clearly the first woman to drive a car across the United States, quite a few newspapers reported that distinction belonged to a 25-year-old motorist named Blanche Stuart Scott (standing, above). Born in Rochester, New York, Scott set out for the West Coast from New York City on May 16, 1910, almost a year after Ramsey. It was to be the second crossing by a female driver, but press releases from Scott's sponsor, the Willys-Overland Company, boldly declared it was the first.

Scott drove her white, 25-horsepower Overland to San Francisco in 68 days, stopping frequently to make public appearances at Overland dealerships. At a time when many women were still being encouraged to drive electric vehicles, the company hoped Scott's achievement would show them the durability and appeal of gasoline cars. One of the highlights of Scott's trip was a Memorial Day visit to the Indianapolis Motor Speedway to watch the inaugural races on its new brick surface. When famed driver Barney Oldfield let Scott take a spin around the track in his car, she was thrilled to attain a speed of 80 miles per hour.

Later that year, Scott took flying lessons and logged the first solo flight by a woman. She became a professional pilot, earning the nickname "Tomboy of the Air" as she flew upside down in stunt exhibitions and tested prototypes of new planes. Scott eventually quit the business and turned to screenwriting, working in Hollywood for 14 years. She also wrote and appeared on radio shows and helped collect artifacts for an aviation museum. Blanche Stuart Scott died on January 12, 1970, at age 84.

soon see more equal suffragists taking the suit case [*sic*]
and the automobile," the paper
wrote in an editorial, "and faring
forth to talk to the unconverted
men of the state." When Illinois
voted in 1913 to allow women to cast
ballots in presidential and municipal
elections, McCulloch credited the auto
tours as "one of the great causes of our
final victory."

Also in 1913, motorists became an
important ingredient in the push for a constitu-
tional amendment that would enfranchise women
throughout the country. In March a huge suffrage
parade in Washington, D.C., on the eve of Woodrow
Wilson's presidential inauguration resulted in
chaos, as crowds of men interfered with the
demonstrators. Undaunted, the National American
Woman Suffrage Association (NAWSA) planned
an even more dramatic rally that summer. The
group directed delegates from all 48 states to
collect signatures on petitions supporting a
suffrage amendment and bring them to the
nation's capital. Mrs. G.H. Robertson of Jackson,
Tennessee, carried hers in a new automobile
that her husband gave her. Jeannette Rankin,
who in 1916 would become the first woman
elected to the U.S. Congress, drove hers all
the way from Butte, Montana. On July 31, more

**The equal suffragists who are auto-
mobiling through northwestern Illinois
seem to have found at last the road
which may lead to victory."** —"Equal
Suffrage Missionaries," *Chicago Daily
Tribune*, July 2, 1910

Catherine Waugh McCulloch (far right) is embraced
by a suffragist after Illinois granted women the right
to vote in some elections in 1913.

Inset: A pro-suffrage pin from the early twentieth century

VOTES FOR WOMEN

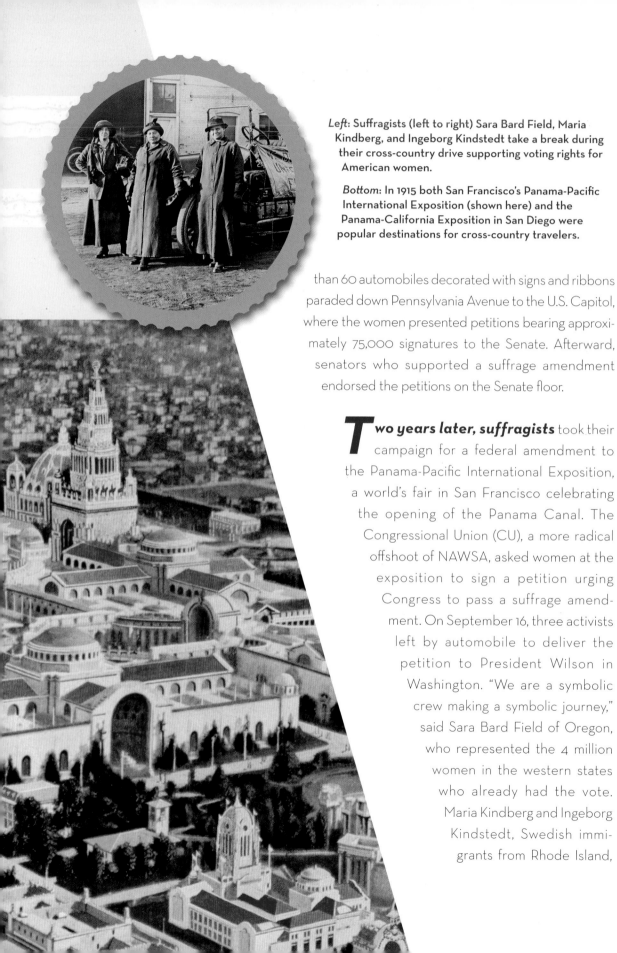

Left: Suffragists (left to right) Sara Bard Field, Maria Kindberg, and Ingeborg Kindstedt take a break during their cross-country drive supporting voting rights for American women.

Bottom: In 1915 both San Francisco's Panama-Pacific International Exposition (shown here) and the Panama-California Exposition in San Diego were popular destinations for cross-country travelers.

than 60 automobiles decorated with signs and ribbons paraded down Pennsylvania Avenue to the U.S. Capitol, where the women presented petitions bearing approximately 75,000 signatures to the Senate. Afterward, senators who supported a suffrage amendment endorsed the petitions on the Senate floor.

Two years later, suffragists took their campaign for a federal amendment to the Panama-Pacific International Exposition, a world's fair in San Francisco celebrating the opening of the Panama Canal. The Congressional Union (CU), a more radical offshoot of NAWSA, asked women at the exposition to sign a petition urging Congress to pass a suffrage amendment. On September 16, three activists left by automobile to deliver the petition to President Wilson in Washington. "We are a symbolic crew making a symbolic journey," said Sara Bard Field of Oregon, who represented the 4 million women in the western states who already had the vote. Maria Kindberg and Ingeborg Kindstedt, Swedish immigrants from Rhode Island, symbolized the 20 million American women without the vote. They provided the car for the trip and served as driver and mechanic, respectively. The petition they carried was a rolled-up scroll 18,333 feet (over three miles) long that had more than 500,000 signatures at the start of their journey. Field gave speeches at rallies as the trio drove across the country and collected even more signatures, including those of politicians who supported their cause.

Though Field and her party did meet with President Wilson in Washington, he said only that he would consider the issue. So in 1916, with the presidential nominating conventions set for summer, suffragists again took to the road to urge the Democrats and Republicans to add a suffrage plank to their party platforms. NAWSA sent Alice Burke and Nell Richardson on a complete loop around the country. The women traveled 10,700 miles over six months in their sturdy yellow Saxon Four roadster, along with a kitten they appropriately named Saxon. It was the longest suffrage ride and one of the last. When the 19th Amendment was ratified in 1920, finally giving all female U.S. citizens the right to vote in all elections, the impact of the automobile on the fight for suffrage could not be denied. ⚙

Reprinted from *Automobile Topics* weekly magazine

NEW YORK, NY · OCTOBER 23, 1915

ANITA KING COMPLETES TRANSCONTINENTAL TRIP ALONE IN A KISSEL

A total of 5,231 miles, made in a Kissel driven all by herself, is the record of Anita King, of moving picture fame, whose arrival in New York City on Wednesday of this week, terminated a trip across the continent. Miss King, whose face and name are known to thousands who follow the moving pictures, left the Pacific Coast with greetings from the mayors of San Francisco and Los Angeles, to be given to Mayor Mitchel, of New York. She drove through Wyoming, Utah, Nebraska and then to Chicago, after which she circled around through New York State before driving to Asbury Park and to Philadelphia, the last named place being where she came from to New York.

Not all of the credit is due Miss King, however, for the performance of the Kissel Kar which she drove was most remarkable, considering the fact that no mechanician or other person accompanied Miss King and the car on the long journey.

CORONATION VEIL

The most practical, becoming and convenient veil designed for the Automobilist. It may be worn equally well over a dressy hat or Auto-cap. Gives complete protection from dust and holds hat firmly in position. Passes round the neck, and ties with a neat flowing bow.

No. 409. Light Silk Material. Price, $4.50. Our Price, $

"BUR

WATERPR

—

Exceptiona coats, cut fro have all the out the ob tures of r u present a fas ance, and suited for mo

No. 888. Drab fully cut that is w comfort.

No. 889. Drab with thic Warm as worn with Pr

RU____ T GOGGLES

Guaranteed Waterproof

A Sure Protection in Stormy Weather

Made of fin rubber. Goes Neck is fitte when fastened

No. 440. Black 50 in. long. Price, $

No. 442. Bl Price, $

No. 890. Da Red feather rich garment

THE WELL-DRESSED MOTORIST

It's no wonder early motorists wore protective gear. As they rode in open cars, they were bombarded by dust, wind, rain, and snow. Before long, their practical needs caught the imagination of fashion designers, leading *Motor* magazine to declare, "Fashion has a new and most exacting mistress in the motor girl." Here's what the well-dressed motor girl and boy and even dog were wearing in the first decade of the twentieth century.

CAPES AND PONCHOS

No. 502. Cape,

No. 949. "Boreas." Crave nose-piece, unlined. with chenille. Price, $

No. 950. "Boreas." Crave

> **HATS AND HOODS:**
Early motorists seemed always to cover their heads, and often their headgear had a strap or tie under the chin to keep it from blowing away. Among the many options: men's hoods that looked like gas masks; women's hoods with veils covering their faces; jaunty caps for men; flowery hats for women; leather hats; fur hats; and rubber caps to repel rain and snow.

> **GOGGLES:** Gearing up for a drive often meant putting on goggles to keep dust, dirt, and insects out of one's eyes. Some models were plain, like swimmer's goggles. Others were bejeweled, while still others had leather or silk attached to cover the nose and mouth as well as the eyes.

> **COATS AND DUSTERS:** Motorists could choose from coats of different weights, lengths, materials, styles, and price points. In warm weather, when coats would be stifling, men and women could wear loose-fitting linen dusters that fastened at the neck and around the sleeves to protect clothing from dust. On rainy days, motorists could don rubber raincoats, some of which were wide enough to fit over the car's steering wheel as well.

> **GLOVES AND GAUNTLETS:** Drivers wore gloves both to keep their hands warm in winter and to grip the steering wheel year-round. Depending on the season and the weather, drivers chose gloves made of fur, leather, rubber, or silk. Gauntlets, or gloves with large cuffs at the top, protected drivers' sleeves as well as their hands.

> **LEGGINGS AND FOOT PROTECTORS:** Early automobiles were open to the elements and had no heaters, so drivers and passengers went to great lengths to keep their legs and feet warm. Men could wear leather leggings, which provided an extra layer from the ankle to the calf. Women could stick their feet into fur-lined foot muffs or use a fur lap robe, which wrapped around the body and sometimes had slots for their feet.

Pages from a 1907 catalog advertise ladies' hats and goggles and men's outerwear, while a dog sports a scarf, coat, and goggles for an early twentieth-century car ride.

CHAPTER 4

The Need for Speed

In 1918 Bessie Oldfield, wife of racing champ Barney Oldfield, waves the flag to start a women's auto race at Ascot Park in California.

❝ O Mrs. Cuneo, O Mrs. Cuneo,
The greatest woman driver that we know,
She keeps a-going; she makes a showing,
Does Mrs. Cuney, uney, uney O."
—Song sung by racing fans in Boston, 1908

Barney Oldfield was America's first great automobile racing champion, but he met his match in Joan Newton Cuneo. Oldfield initially encountered Cuneo in September 1905 at the Dutchess County Fair in Poughkeepsie, New York. Both were there to compete on a dirt track that was usually home to horse races. This was Cuneo's first experience racing on a track—most auto races were held on public roads or flat beaches at the time—and she took to it quickly. "It was a case of love at first sight," she would later write, "and my love for track driving increased each time I drove around one." Oldfield was curious about the 29-year-old mother of two and accepted an invitation to be a passenger while she took a few practice laps. But he wasn't prepared for how competitive Cuneo's practice laps could be. With his heart in his throat as they tore around the oval, Oldfield finally felt compelled to blurt out "Slow down!"

During the early years of the twentieth century, Joan Newton Cuneo rarely slowed down. From her first races in 1905 to her last almost a decade later, Cuneo was the most dominant female automobile racer in the United States. She participated in "reliability tours," long-distance races over mostly unpaved roads that were meant to show the public how reliable the motor car could be. She competed in hill climbs, steering her car up steep elevations with

Above: Joan Newton Cuneo pilots her Rainier in the 1,669-mile, 15-day Glidden Tour endurance race in 1908.

Below: Cuneo competes in the women's race from New York to Philadelphia and back in January 1909. The rules allowed each driver to bring a female passenger. Cuneo was one of 12 drivers—and ultimately finished first.

switchbacks and hairpin turns. She raced against and often beat men on circular tracks, going a total of 5, 10, or 50 miles. And she flew through speed trials, repeatedly lowering the record for the fastest mile driven by a woman until she reached her best mark: 1 minute and 1/5 second. In 1910 *Outing* magazine declared that Cuneo had "won more motoring prizes for speed,

endurance, and skill than any other woman alive." Her achievements even brought her product endorsements. In magazine ads, she praised the durability and "marvelous riding qualities" of Renault automobiles and celebrated the ease of using the Ward Leonard self-starter instead of a hand crank.

59

While **Cuneo was unique** in her success as an early female race car driver in the United States, she had two notable counterparts overseas. Camille du Gast of France started racing in 1901. Dorothy Levitt of Great Britain began two years later. Like Cuneo, both distinguished themselves against male opponents and never shrank from a challenge. But the three women also shared a more dubious distinction. Each was ultimately banned from competing in the sport she loved.

When Camille du Gast started racing, European events ran from city to city on public roads. She entered her first race, the 1901 contest from Paris, France, to Berlin, Germany, in a bulky 20-horsepower motor car rather than a proper race car. One of two women in the competition, she started last in a field of 122 entrants, but finished 33rd. (The other woman did not finish.) Du Gast's next significant race was the 1903 run from Paris to Madrid, Spain, which turned out to be one of the most tragic episodes in the history of the sport. The large field of 170 cars and 54 motorcycles, the dry conditions that gave rise to

In 1903 Camille du Gast drives a Benz Parsifal race car designed by her passenger, Marius Barbarou.

Above: Dorothy Levitt takes the controls of a 26-horsepower Napier race car in 1908.

Background: Actress and racing enthusiast Elinor Blevins powers around the Benning Race Track in Washington, D.C., in 1916.

clouds of thick dust on the dirt roadways, and the massive crowds of spectators resulted in horrific accidents all along the way. In the end, five racers and three spectators were killed, many others were injured, and half of all the cars either crashed or retired before the race was halted at Bordeaux, France. Du Gast, who was among the leaders, emerged unscathed. In fact, she stopped racing long enough to help another driver who had crashed and was credited by some with saving his life. But the horrors of the day would have an unexpected impact on her.

Despite du Gast's heroic performance, the governing body for automobile racing in France voted to ban women from its future contests. "The rule was obviously made to keep Mme. du Gast from participating," wrote one newspaper in the United States. Some cast it as a defensive move. The calamities at the Paris-Madrid race were bad enough, they suggested, but if a *woman* driver were injured or killed in a subsequent race, there surely would be calls to outlaw all automobile competitions. And indeed, those who felt women were naturally nervous behind the wheel expected that such an accident eventually would occur. Du Gast protested the decision and claimed the men in charge were envious of her success. "Chivalry is flying from France and jealousy is taking its place," she declared. But she didn't wait around for the policy to change. She washed her hands of automobile contests and started racing motorboats instead.

Though women were forbidden from racing in France, they could still do so in Great Britain, and Dorothy Levitt quickly made a name for herself there. In 1903 Levitt was a 21-year-old secretary at Napier and Son, manufacturers of Napier automobiles. Selwyn Edge, who raced and sold Napiers and other cars, saw how much publicity Camille du Gast was attracting and reportedly handpicked Levitt to represent his brands on the racetrack. Although Levitt had never even driven an automobile at the time, she was a fast learner. Before the year was out, she had beaten all the cars in her class (based on their price range) at the speed races at Southport, England, winning a silver cup. The following year she

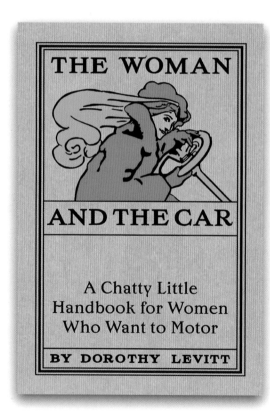

THE WOMAN AND THE CAR

A Chatty Little Handbook for Women Who Want to Motor

BY DOROTHY LEVITT

Osprey Publishing, a British company, reprinted Levitt's book with this cover and a revised subtitle in 2014.

competed in the Hereford 1,000-mile marathon race, losing only because she had to take time out to repair a faulty valve in her carburetor. But she returned to Southport in 1904 and won two medals.

Levitt entered a variety of speed and distance events over the next several years. She set and broke her own women's world speed record—ultimately reaching her fastest mark of 96 miles per hour—and beat Camille du Gast in one of the Frenchwoman's last races. But when Great Britain's first track for automobile racing, Brooklands, opened in 1907, officials refused to allow women to compete against men there. By the time they decided to stage a women-only "Ladies' Bracelet Handicap" in 1908, Levitt had moved on, concentrating on hill climbs and long-distance races in England and elsewhere in Europe. She also was busy writing a series of articles and then a book about driving for women. *The Woman and the Car: A Chatty Little Handbook for All Women Who Motor or Who Want to Motor*, published in 1909, promised to deliver "simple and understandable instructions and hints for all women motorists, whether beginners or experts." Among other advice, she suggested that drivers should keep a mirror handy "to occasionally hold up to see what is behind you." This was one of the

Reprinted from *Motorcycle Illustrated* monthly magazine

NEW YORK, NY • MARCH 1, 1909

SOMETHING TO BE AVOIDED

Mrs. Smith, motorcycle enthusiast

A women's automobile race has been held in New Orleans. Decent, self-respecting automobilists decry the proposition, and hope this will be the end of it. No similar effort has as yet been made in motorcycling. The competition rules of the F.A.M. expressly prohibit this sort of thing, and every sound-minded motorcyclist is in sympathy with the prohibition. It would be too much, however, to feel entirely confident that the effort will never be made. The opportunity to create an unseemly sensation is more than likely to prove too great a temptation to some unprincipled promoter. If so, an accident will follow as a matter of course, public indignation will be properly aroused, and the excellent effects of much missionary work nullified. Of course, motorcyclists will do all in their power to prevent such an unfortunate consummation.

Note: The F.A.M. was the Federation of American Motorcyclists, formed in 1903 to encourage the use of motorcycles, oversee motorcycle competitions, and fight local ordinances restricting motorcycle riding.

63

first introductions to the concept of the rearview mirror, which would be patented by Chester A. Weed of Brooklyn, New York, in 1914.

With *France banning women* from motor car racing and England's lone track severely limiting their participation, it's not surprising that officials in the United States started weighing the future of female competitors. Early in 1909, U.S. automobile manufacturers agreed to give the American Automobile Association (AAA) the authority to oversee track racing. Without any fanfare, this alliance of auto clubs added a rule that only males were eligible to participate in its contests. This left Joan

Nell Shipman

Anyone searching for a bold, independent heroine in the era of silent films had to look no further than Nell Shipman. As a writer, producer, director, and star, Shipman was responsible for more than two dozen independent films that revolved around strong women succeeding against all odds. At least two of them showcased leading ladies with extraordinary skills behind the wheel of an automobile.

Both *Something New* and *Trail of the Arrow* were paid for by automobile manufacturers, but rather than filming glorified commercials, Shipman wrote stories of daring women who saved the day in their cars. Reviewers called the former picture, a romantic adventure tale featuring a Maxwell, "the fastest and most dashing depiction of an automobile in action ever made."

But they were even more enthusiastic about the latter, centered on two women who drove an Essex Arrow across the rough terrain of California's Mojave Desert to win a $1,000 wager. The critic for the *San Francisco Chronicle* wrote, "It is the most sensational motor-car picture ever screened and simply goes to show that the woman driver of today is perfectly competent to handle an automobile anywhere the car can be driven."

Shipman made both films in 1920, two years after barely surviving a bout with Spanish flu during the worldwide pandemic (see pages 81 to 83). Born in Vancouver, British Columbia, Canada, she also co-wrote and starred in the most successful Canadian silent film ever made, 1919's *Back to God's Country*. She died in 1970 at age 77.

Newton Cuneo and all other women racers out in the cold. As in France, some people blamed the change on fears that an accident involving a woman would bring down the public's wrath upon the sport. The *Washington Post* expressed that opinion a year before the new rule took effect. "Should Cuneo meet with a serious accident, a wave of horror would go through the community," the paper predicted, "and the committee would be severely censured for permitting a woman to take part in the contest." But there were other factors as well. Automobile racing was evolving from a somewhat genteel amateur sport to a more cutthroat professional one, and many people felt it was improper for women to take part. What's more, professional racers had a financial stake in the ban. Losing to a woman would be a blow not only to their egos but also to their wallets.

> **❝ Mamma doesn't want me to take any risks, but dear mamma doesn't know that it is perfectly safe to drive a car fast when you know the roads perfectly."** – Katherine Drexel Dahlgren, the *Evening Telegram*, New York, January 8, 1917

65

Reprinted from the *New York Times* daily newspaper

NEW YORK, NY • OCTOBER 18, 1915

SPEED COSTS HER LICENSE.

Miss Katherine Dahlgren Barred from Bay State Roads.

Lenox, Mass. — After investigating many complaints against Miss Katherine Dahlgren of New York, driver of a 110 horse power [*sic*] racing automobile, the State Highway Commission has suspended her license.

She was three times in the Lee District Court on charges of speeding, operating her automobile in a dangerous manner, and driving the car with the muffler cut off. She was fined on two charges, the rest being filed.

Miss Dahlgren is a daughter of Mrs. Drexel Dahlgren. She is 20 years old, and has owned the racing automobile since Spring. Her dashes through the Brookshires at high speed were the sensation of the early season, and led to complaints from citizens in many communities.

In June 1903, *Le Petit Journal*, a French newspaper, published this print depicting the tragedies that befell participants in that year's Paris to Madrid road race.

After the AAA ban, women in the United States were only welcome at exhibitions, speed trials—where they raced against the clock rather than other people—and the occasional small-town competition that defied the organization's rules. But just as fearless female motorists started to disappear from the racing circuit, they began to have an increased presence in motion pictures. Close to a dozen silent films revolving around heroic women drivers were made in the United States between 1908 and 1921, and the actresses who starred in them seemed as passionate about automobiles as their characters. In fact, reviewers of some films seemed more likely to praise the protagonists' driving than their acting. In the 1914 movie *The President's Special,* a telegraph operator failed to warn the conductor of a train full of children that he was headed for a collision with the president's train. His quick-thinking wife jumped into her

Model T and raced to warn the conductor, who stopped the train just in time. In its review, the *Washington Herald* pointed out that actress Gertrude McCoy "drove her own car in this spirited chase with a skill and display of nerve that carried her into the front ranks of girls who dare and do more than the average man would attempt or accomplish under the same circumstances."

Although movie motorists were several steps removed from the real female stars of the racetrack, both showed that women could rival men as daredevils and heroes. Filmmaker Nell Shipman, who starred in two of the most dramatic motorist movies, said as much. "Woman is on a par with man in driving a motor car, as she is in every other walk of life. The ability is there. All she needs is the experience." It was a pertinent message as American women fought for the vote and, starting in 1914, watched Europe becoming engulfed in war. Even before the United States entered the fighting in 1917, the war would give women the opportunity to volunteer their skills as motorists at home and abroad. Soon the fearless, female driver would be delivering supplies and maneuvering ambulances, using her skills not to win a race, but to help win a war. ✻

Above: Silent film star Gertrude McCoy

Below: In *Something New*, Nell Shipman is a passenger until her male companion is injured and she saves the day with her driving skills.

67

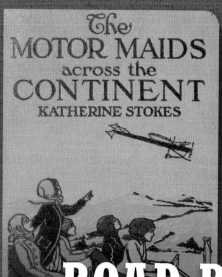

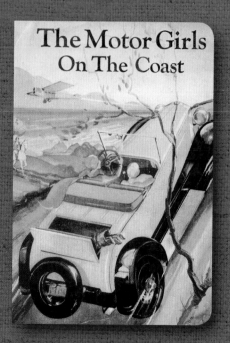

ROAD READS

As automobiles became increasingly prominent on America's roads, they became equally prominent in the books that young people read. Starting in 1906, several multibook series for girls and boys centered around the adventures of middle-class friends and their motor cars.

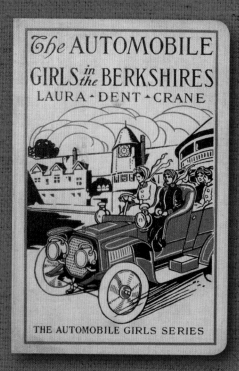

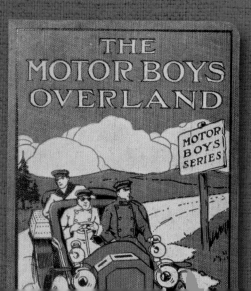

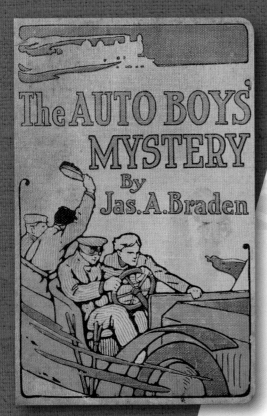

> **THE MOTOR BOYS:**
With 22 books published from
1906 through 1924, this was the
most successful motor series.
The stories, "telling the doings of
a number of lively, up-to-date lads,"
included exploits with motorcycles,
boats, and airplanes, as well as cars.

> **THE AUTO BOYS:** This
series, introduced in 1908, followed
the adventures of "four healthy, vigor-
ous, ambitious boys who decide to own
an automobile." It promised to be "of
utmost interest to every boy who delights
in automobiles, and where is there one
who does not?"

> **THE AUTOMOBILE GIRLS:**
"There is no room for doubt that these are the
most interesting stories ever penned for girls,"
boasted an ad for this series. Premiering in 1910
the series followed a quartet of high school girls
and their adult chaperone to various locations in
the United States.

> **THE MOTOR GIRLS:** Published starting
in 1910 by the same group responsible for The Motor
Boys (and later Nancy Drew), this series chronicled
the automobile tours, vacations, and other adventures
of Cora Kimball and her friends. They were, according
to the publisher, "in the final analysis, just wholesome,
everyday girls."

> **THE MOTOR MAIDS:** "Billie Campbell was
just the type of a straightforward, athletic girl to be successful as a practical Motor Maid," declared an ad for this
series. Beginning in 1911, Billie, her aunt, and her three close
friends chased adventure across the country and all the way
to England and Japan.

Book series abounded in the early twentieth century, and the final
pages of most volumes included rundowns of other offerings for
eager readers. Additional series for girls included the Camp Fire
Girls, the Meadow-Brook Girls, and the Tucker Twins. Boys could
follow the Baseball Joe series, the Speedwell Boys, and the
Submarine Boys, among many others.

CHAPTER 5

Driving for Liberty

New ambulance drivers in Washington, D.C., get a hands-on lesson under the hood in 1920.

❝ The woman who was afraid to go out after dark to mail a letter may have a granddaughter who is on her way to France to drive an ambulance ... It's a long way that women have come, and we stand at salute as they go by."—Anne Lewis Pierce, *New-York Tribune*, October 21, 1917

In 1918 Mary Dexter regularly maneuvered motor vehicles through France in conditions that would make even the most daring cross-country driver balk. "I was the night-driver on duty," Dexter wrote to her mother on March 24, 1918. "The guns were just starting as I left here ... Some bombs fell very near just as I got to the H.O.E. [Evacuation Hospital] and the noise was deafening. I had just stopped my engine, preparatory to beating it for cover, when shrapnel whizzed past my head." Dexter, a minister's daughter from Massachusetts, was a trained nurse who volunteered her services soon after war broke out in Europe in 1914. Following nursing assignments in Great Britain and Belgium, she passed a driving test and a mechanic's exam and became an ambulance driver. During six months with a private ambulance unit attached to the French Army, she transported injured soldiers as war raged around her.

Dexter captured her experiences in frequent letters to her mother, who in turn edited them into the book *In the Soldier's Service*. She was one of thousands of Americans who volunteered to aid the Allied Powers, led by Great Britain, France, and Russia, in the ever escalating war against the Central Powers, led by Germany and Austria-Hungary. Although President Woodrow Wilson vowed to keep the United States out of the hostilities of this "Great War," idealistic individuals followed their hearts and sense of adventure to Europe, eager to contribute. In February 1915 a 27-year-old Harvard graduate named Edward Mandell Stone became the first American killed in action as he fought alongside the French.

American women living in Europe and those who came specifically to support the Allies could drive for the British or French branches of the Red Cross or one of several other relief groups. These early volunteers generally were financially well-off, and many donated their own automobiles to the cause. Author Gertrude Stein, who lived in Paris, joined the American Fund for French Wounded (AFFW), which ferried injured soldiers and delivered supplies to hospitals in France. Driving was new to Stein, but she gamely learned the basics while waiting for a cousin in New York to buy her a Model T and ship it to her. Once the car arrived, she named it "Auntie" after her Aunt Pauline, who, she wrote, "always behaved admirably in emergencies and behaved fairly well most times if she was properly flattered." The Ford lived up

Above: Nurses Mairi Chisholm (left) and Elsie Knocker of Great Britain drive an ambulance through the bombed-out battle zone of Pervyse, Belgium, in 1917.

Right: American ambulance driver Mary Dexter

> **War compels women to work. That is one of its merits. Women are forced to use body and mind, they are not, cannot be idlers."**
> —Harriot Stanton Blatch,
> *Mobilizing Woman-Power*, 1918

to Aunt Pauline's example, and Stein celebrated her newfound mobility by offering a lift to any soldier she passed on the road.

Even when bombs were not falling around them, the women who drove for the Allies had to contend with conditions that were a far cry from their privileged lives back home. The May 1918 issue of *Motor* magazine reported on the experiences of one such "crusader of mercy," an unnamed American woman who was finishing her training as a mechanic before going to the front. "I wish you could see me now," the woman wrote to a friend. "The mud is ten inches deep here, and after four hours under my car making repairs I am literally unrecognizable." She went on to describe her living quarters, a small curtained-off area in a wooden barracks that never had hot water and often had no water at all. "In severe weather like now, due to the cold, we don't undress for a week," she wrote. "Once a week we get leave to go into the village for a bath." Rather than discouraging the writer, however, these hardships seemed to inspire her. "I love it," she told her friend. "I who have always loved my lap of luxury. Can you imagine it?"

Opportunities for American women to support the Allied cause increased greatly in January 1917 with the formation of the National League for Women's Service (NLWS). It was a response to two ominous signs of increased

Left: Lolita Coffin Van Rensselaer, vice chairman of the NLWS, believed that in wartime it was up to American women to provide "a national morale without which we cannot have the sure victory."

German aggression. First, despite warnings from President Wilson, German U-boats (submarines) were ramping up attacks on American commercial ships and ocean liners with U.S. citizens onboard. Then Great Britain shared a telegram they intercepted from Germany's foreign minister, Arthur Zimmermann, to that nation's ambassador to Mexico, Heinrich von Eckardt. The telegram instructed von Eckardt that if the U.S. entered the war, he should invite Mexico to join the Central Powers. In turn, Germany would promise to help Mexico win back former Mexican territory in Texas, Arizona, and New Mexico. Mexico ultimately remained neutral. But when Wilson

Charles Dana Gibson, illustrator of the vibrant, modern Gibson Girl in turn-of-the-century magazines, created this and other posters during World War I.

read the German telegram, he determined that the U.S. must enter the conflict to make the world "safe for democracy." He said as much to Congress on April 2, 1917. Four days later, the legislative body voted to declare war on Germany.

As American troops mobilized to fight overseas, their wives, mothers, sisters, and daughters mobilized on the home front. The NLWS had anticipated the need for female workers after studying the contributions to the war being made by women in Great Britain and France. "It was the first national war organization with a complete program and it attempted to solve the problem of the volunteer from every angle," wrote Lolita Coffin Van Rensselaer, vice chairman of the organization. The National League recruited women to help in several areas. A social and welfare division ran recreational canteens

for soldiers and sailors. An agricultural group worked with another civilian organization, the Women's Land Army of America, to teach women how to grow community gardens. A home economics division shared methods of food conservation, so as to leave more food for the troops. A general services division provided a variety of volunteers, including bookkeepers, translators, office staff, and workers for Liberty [savings] Bond drives. By the time Congress declared war on Germany, the National League had approximately 50,000 members in 31 states. By September 1918, it had expanded to 300,000 members in 41 states.

Left: This Women's Motor Corps member is in full uniform, complete with a garrison cap.

Below Right: Women's Motor Corps drivers stand at the ready with their ambulances.

Automobiles at War

In 1915 the *Lotus* magazine, a New York–based publication, boldly declared that if not for the automobile, Paris would have fallen to the Central Powers during the first weeks of the Great War. The Army of Paris requisitioned every automobile in the city to transport supplies and troops to the battlefield, the magazine explained. Based on that alone, "it has practically wrought a revolution."

From there, according to the *Lotus*, motor vehicles continued to transform warfare, especially in the delivery of supplies. A truck could carry more than a horse-drawn carriage, travel faster, and keep going as long as it had fuel. On the other hand, horses had to be housed and fed and could cover only 10 to 15 miles each day before being replaced with a fresh team. The efficiency of motor vehicles was so great that some troops could be supplied with fresh meat and bread instead of relying on canned products.

Besides supply trucks, the Great War also saw motor vehicles fitted with water tanks, soup kitchens, x-ray machines, traveling bathrooms, and even portable operating rooms, bringing medical care and other services closer to where they were needed.

From the start, the National League's Women's Motor Corps was one of its busiest and most successful divisions. "The organizers of the League have always believed that motor driving was an essential job in which the women could release the much-needed men," wrote Van Rensselaer. Each driver wore a khaki uniform with a skirt, a belted

> **❝ Many of us are beginning to realize that the ownership of a car is not only a luxury but an opportunity as well.**" —Mrs. Caspar Whitney, *The Delineator*, May 1920

Norfolk jacket, leather leggings, and a cap with a visor or a flat, foldable garrison cap. Like their counterparts overseas, drivers had to pass a mechanics exam. They also had to learn first aid—undergoing complete training in diagnosing illnesses and injuries—and become familiar with the basics of military communications using Morse code and signal flags. Plus they participated in infantry drills. "We cover all of the army drill except the manual of arms," said Captain Helen Bastedo, national chairman of the motor division of the NLWS, "as we do not carry guns. The work is intensive."

77

Reprinted from the *Automobile* weekly magazine

NEW YORK, NY • JUNE 28, 1917

WOMEN WORKING IN FACTORIES

DETROIT, June 25—Planning to meet the labor shortage which will be produced by prolonged war, the automobile industry is beginning to regard women seriously for factory work. At present approximately 3,000 women are being employed in the factory of the Chalmers Motor Co., the Aluminum Castings Co., Morgan & Wright, the Maxwell Motor Co. and the General Brass & Aluminum Co. The Chalmers Motor Co. is making a very extensive experiment and has placed women on drill presses, bench machines, milling machines, assembling machines and inspecting, and is also using them in the foundry. Various manufacturers, now figuring on the employment of women, contemplate placing them in such occupations as sorters, counters, inspectors, sweepers, cleaners, punch press operators, screw machine work, threading and tapping screws, bench assembling and core making.

Women work in a factory assembling magnetos, which used magnets to provide pulses of electric current to power a car's spark plugs.

Motor Corps members performed a whole host of duties. In New York City a driver was regularly assigned to follow each truck that carried war relief supplies from a warehouse to a ship waiting to take them overseas. If the truck was delayed, it was the Motor Corps driver's responsibility to hurry ahead and alert a tugboat, which would in turn tell the ship to wait. In Lansing, Michigan, Motor Corps drivers picked up nine three-quarter-ton trucks at the Reo Motor Car factory and successfully drove them 1,014 miles over 10 days to Atlanta, Georgia. It was, according to the *New York Times*, "the first time in history that a truck drive-away has been attempted by women."

A'Lelia Walker

A'Lelia Walker was very much her mother's daughter. Her mom, known professionally as Madam C.J. Walker, was a self-made millionaire who created a revolutionary line of cosmetics and hair care products for black women. In 1906, when she was just 21, A'Lelia took over the company's mail order and manufacturing divisions while her mother worked on expanding the business.

During World War I, many American institutions were segregated—including the armed forces. Determined to support African-American soldiers, Walker became one of 40 members of the only Colored Women's Motor Corps under the sponsorship of the National League for Women's Service. Based in New York, members transported wounded soldiers to hospitals when they arrived from overseas. They also took soldiers to church, ball games, and other diversions as they recovered from illnesses or injuries. African-American newspapers imagined "the surprise and joy of colored soldiers lying wounded in New York hospitals, at [the] sight of women of their own race to comfort and cheer them." The corps ferried people from senior citizen homes and civilian hospitals as well and even accompanied 4,000 orphans to an amusement park.

Walker helped run the Madam C.J. Walker Manufacturing Company after her mother died in 1919. At the same time, she became immersed in the lively cultural reawakening that came to be known as the Harlem Renaissance. She frequently hosted artists, musicians, and literary figures at her New York City townhouse. She died of a cerebral hemorrhage in 1931 at age 46.

❝ The motor corps was on a 24-hour tour of duty last week and met all demands. If our soldiers are to be praised for their manly qualities, the young women also ought to be praised for their spirit of service."—"The American 'Doughgirls,'" *New York Times*, October 1, 1918

The women started each morning at seven and stayed on the road until they reached that night's destination, sometimes as late as 9:30 p.m. "The service of women chauffeurs," wrote the *Times*, "is very acceptable, as it is constantly becoming more difficult to obtain crews of reliable men for these long distance deliveries." The *Times* noted that Motor Corps drivers in New York were taking lessons in truck management to prepare for future missions.

While only a small percentage of Motor Corps members were assigned to drive ambulances overseas, members worked with the Army, Navy, Secret Service, and other government entities on the home front. At the end of 1917, the corps became independent of the National League for Women's Service, and the scope of its work seemed to expand even more. Members provided the transportation at Marine Corps

Besides sponsoring a Colored Women's Motor Corps, the NLWS also operated this canteen for African-American servicemen returning from war.

Reprinted from the *Pittsburgh Post* daily newspaper

PITTSBURGH, PA • JANUARY 19, 1918

WOMEN DRIVE TRUCKS.

WITH THE AMERICAN ARMY IN FRANCE, Jan. 18.—American women motor car drivers have made their appearance in the zone of the army. A few of them are driving big motor trucks for the Y.M.C.A. and are proving their efficiency.

During a recent heavy snowstorm two trucks driven by young women were sliding along a winding road, carrying supplies to a hut from a depot, when they came upon a big French lorry stalled in a ditch. The French soldier in charge of the vehicle was tinkering with the engine, having stalled it while attempting to pull the lorry into the road again. He was having little success.

The women, in short skirts, high and heavy leather boots and woolen caps down over their ears, climbed from their seats and between them managed to start the engine in the stalled lorry. One of them then took the place behind the wheel and by skillful maneuvering brought the lorry out of the ditch. The French driver stood at one side during the operation and watched the women with astonishment.

Note: "Lorry" is the word for "truck" in Great Britain and some other nations.

recruiting drives. They were called upon to chauffeur foreign diplomats and guard female military prisoners. Captain Bastedo trained some members in the techniques for doing thorough body searches, which they put to the test on suspicious women arriving on ships from overseas and at least one group of German women who were headed home. "The only thing we didn't have," the captain reported, "was the chemical tests for sympathetic writing [invisible ink] on the skin. I don't believe we left out anything else."

By November 11, 1918, all of the Central Powers had surrendered, and the war was over. But drivers were needed for a new fight. Thanks in part to troop movements during the war, a deadly strain of the H1N1 influenza (or flu) virus spread quickly around the world, infecting 500 million people and killing between 50 and 100 million in 1918 and 1919. As the flu took hold in the United States, Motor Corps members put their own health at risk to help those who were ill. There were 297 branches across the country at that point, with a total membership of 11,604. And they did whatever needed to be done—transporting patients, cooking meals and scrubbing floors for those who were ill, and even conducting funerals. "Fearless of the possibility of contracting influenza themselves, the Motor Corps women worked night and day, serving frequently as much as 100 hours per week apiece," reported the *Red Cross Bulletin.* "No assignment was refused."

With their heroic efforts during and after the war, the members of the Motor Corps added to the accumulating evidence that a woman could show as much skill and nerve behind the wheel as any man. Contrary to their detractors from the turn of the century, women had proved themselves capable of driving and repairing motor vehicles of every sort. And rather than falling apart under difficult circumstances, they had thrived. When American men returned from victory overseas, they found female motorists who were unwilling to loosen their grip on the steering wheel. The auto industry took notice and soon began promoting the "two-car family," with cars for "him" and "her." As the country moved forward into a new decade that promised to bring good times and infinite opportunities, women were no longer passengers, but drivers. ⚙

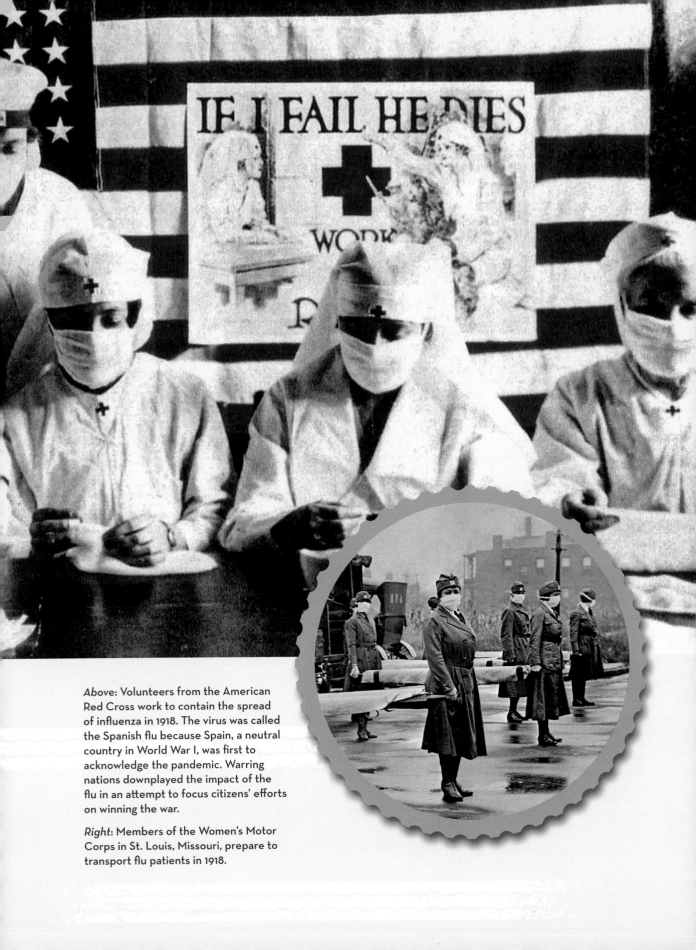

Above: Volunteers from the American Red Cross work to contain the spread of influenza in 1918. The virus was called the Spanish flu because Spain, a neutral country in World War I, was first to acknowledge the pandemic. Warring nations downplayed the impact of the flu in an attempt to focus citizens' efforts on winning the war.

Right: Members of the Women's Motor Corps in St. Louis, Missouri, prepare to transport flu patients in 1918.

MOTORING MILESTONES

While the automobile changed the way people lived and worked, it also had a lasting impact on their surroundings. Here are a few of the "firsts" that led to widespread changes in the American landscape.

MOTEL INN, San Luis Obispo, Cal.
U. S. 101, North City Limits

Architect Arthur Heineman named his business "Milestone Motor Hotel," but he couldn't fit all the letters on the rooftop sign. So he shortened the last two words to "Mo-Tel." By the time this postcard was issued in the 1940s, the name had been changed to Motel Inn.

"America's Motor Lunch"

PIG STANDS, Inc.

DINING ROOM AND
CURB SERVICE

~

Breakfast Menu

~

Open All Night

~

Number 38

4017 Oak Lawn Avenue
DALLAS

Trade Mark Registered

Soon after the first Pig Stand opened, other outlets cropped up in Texas and beyond. This 1938 menu is from Pig Stand #38.

> **AUTO REPAIR SHOP, 1899:** Before W.T. McCullough opened the Back City Cycle and Motor Company in Boston, Massachusetts, a motorist whose vehicle broke down had to return it to the manufacturer for repairs, find a blacksmith, or fix it him- or herself. Besides running his shop, McCullough also built his own gasoline-powered automobile.

> **DRIVE-IN GAS STATION, 1913:** The Gulf Refining Company sold only 30 gallons of gas (at 27 cents a gallon) the Monday it opened its drive-in service station in Pittsburgh, Pennsylvania. But with free air, water, and tire installations, customers couldn't stay away. On its first Saturday the station sold 350 gallons.

> **ELECTRIC TRAFFIC LIGHT, 1914:** The city of Cleveland, Ohio, installed the first electric traffic signal at the intersection of Euclid Avenue and East 105th Street. Operated by an officer inside a control booth, the signal consisted of a pair of red and green lights facing each side of the busy, four-way intersection. When emergency vehicles were approaching, the officer could even turn all the lights red and sound a gong to stop traffic.

> **DRIVE-IN RESTAURANT, 1921:** Motorists in Dallas, Texas, who preferred to eat on the run lucked out when Jesse Kirby and Reuben Jackson opened the Pig Stand restaurant. Drivers parked, honked their horns, and waited for the male attendants to take and then deliver their orders. It was a recipe for success. By 1924 there were 10 Pig Stands in Dallas, serving up a total of 50,000 pork sandwiches per week.

> **MOTEL, 1925:** Early motorists on road trips could pitch their tents at campsites, stay at fancy hotels, or sleep in their cars. But then the Milestone Mo-Tel (short for motor hotel) opened in San Luis Obispo, California. It was a reasonably priced and convenient option for Americans on the go.

Left, background: The first drive-in gasoline station, seen here in 1913, stood at the corner of Baum Boulevard and St. Clair Street in Pittsburgh, Pennsylvania.

Epilogue
Bumpy Roads

In *1931 Charles Coolidge Parlin and Fred Bremier* conducted a comprehensive study of the passenger car industry. One of their most noteworthy findings had to do with the increase in female drivers since their previous study in 1914. They wrote, "We did not dare venture the prophesy that millions of women would be driving and owning cars in 1931, weaving confidently through crowded traffic, driving at express-train speed along the highways." Parlin and Bremier explained this phenomenon by listing several technological innovations they felt made driving a more inviting experience for women. There was the self-starter, of course, which was finally available in most cars by 1920. There also were improvements in steering, gear shifting, tires, and brakes. And then there was the advent of the closed car. By 1931, 92.2 percent of all new cars had closed bodies with hard tops, making driving more comfortable in bad weather.

Of course, these breakthroughs helped male drivers as well as females. But Parlin and Bremier also pointed out a cultural shift that particularly impacted the number of women on the road. "In the War, women went into employment and into social work and when the War was over they did not return to a life of seclusion," they wrote. And indeed, women who had been empowered as ambulance drivers or Motor Corps members had no intention of regressing into timid homebodies. "Modern housewives with a multiplicity of duties outside the home need cars of their own," they concluded.

Automobile manufacturers had no problem providing cars for this expanding market. But the industry, run almost exclusively by men, developed skewed assumptions about who their female customers were and what was important to them. They targeted their advertisements at married women, figuring that those who were single would eventually settle down as well. And rather than focusing on the mechanical attributes of vehicles, as they did in ads aimed at men, they highlighted their cars' aesthetic

❝ Every time a woman learns to drive—and thousands do every year—it is a threat at yesterday's order of things."
—Ray W. Sherman, "The New Buyer," *Motor,* January 1927

This 1970 ad appeals to male consumers who would envy the surfer's quandary of whether to use his car to transport a surfboard or other "great things that tend to congregate" around the vehicle, like a half-dozen bikini-clad women.

qualities. "One of the first things a woman thinks of when the purchase of a new car is considered," reported *Autobody* magazine in 1925, "is whether the color of the upholstering will harmonize with her personality, coloring and clothes. In other words, 'Will she look well in it?'"

As they tried to sell form over function to female customers, many car manufacturers also used images of women in suggestive poses to sell cars to men. These tactics informed the automobile industry's approach to women for much of the twentieth century, undermining the need to treat a growing segment of the market as serious buyers. Stories abounded of car salesmen who continually ignored female consumers and instead addressed the boyfriends or husbands or fathers who accompanied them. In 1925 an informed car shopper named Edith M. Garfield reported that one dealer "made me feel that I should be home playing with paper dolls, leaving such matters as buying

Both Sarah McCune (left) and Danica Patrick had the best qualifying times at their races in Joliet, Illinois, on September 11, 2005, earning the right to start at the pole position, the inside of the front row. Although auto racing remains a sport dominated by men, female competitors are becoming more common on racing circuits in the twenty-first century.

an automobile to a man." And as recently as 2009, a Porsche salesman famously asked Anne Mulcahy, who happened to be the chief executive officer (CEO) of the Xerox Corporation, if she needed to check with someone before leasing a new 911 Cabriolet. She responded by threatening to go to another dealership if the man didn't start the paperwork immediately.

In the twenty-first century, though, the auto industry has seen at least some movement toward gender equality. In 2012 the Women's Business Enterprise Council named Ford one of America's top corporations—the first automobile company to receive that honor—for its growing use of women-owned suppliers. Two years later, Mary Barra took the reins at General Motors and became the first female CEO of a major car manufacturer. And in 2015, a group called Women in Automotive began efforts to help the industry recruit, retain, and develop female employees and leaders. Meanwhile, despite the challenges, any questions about a woman's place behind the wheel have been settled. Since 2005 there have been more female than male drivers in the United States. Though it has been a bumpy road at times, the Motor Girl has finally arrived. ⚙

Appendix

Shifting Gears

A FEW FACTS AND FIGURES FOR THE ROAD

Ten Silent Films Featuring Heroines and Their Cars

1. *An Auto Heroine*, 1908
2. *A Beast at Bay*, 1912*
3. *Mabel at the Wheel*, 1914*
4. *The President's Special*, 1914
5. *The Hazards of Helen*, 1914–1917 (serial)*

   *Part or all of these films are available on YouTube.

6. *The Girl and the Game*, 1915 (serial)
7. *The Danger Girl*, 1916*
8. *Trail of the Arrow*, 1920
9. *Something New*, 1920*
10. *The Speed Girl*, 1921

Bebe Daniels (above), star of *The Speed Girl*, liked to drive fast in real life as well as on the silver screen. She once spent 10 days in jail for speeding, but her stay was unusual. A total of 792 fans came to visit (Daniels kept a guestbook), a furniture store sent in a bed set and rocking chair, and a local restaurant catered three meals a day.

Requirements for Girl Scout Automobiling Merit Badge, 1916

① *Must pass an examination equal to that required to obtain a permit or license to operate an automobile in her community.*

② *Know how to start a motor and be able to do it and be able to explain necessary precautions.*

③ *Know how to extinguish burning oil or gasoline.*

④ *Comply with such requirements as are imposed by body conducting the test for licensing drivers.*

NOTE: This was renamed the Motorist badge in the 1920s and had additional requirements, including possessing a driver's license in your state.

Graphic representation of the 1916 Girl Scout Automobiling merit badge

The 1905 Curved Dash Oldsmobile

U.S. Passenger Car Production, 1900–1920

Year	Total Cars Produced	Top U.S. Car Producer
1900	4,192	Columbia
1901	7,000	Locomobile
1902	9,000	Locomobile
1903	11,235	Oldsmobile
1904	22,130	Oldsmobile
1905	24,250	Oldsmobile
1906	33,200	Ford
1907	43,000	Ford
1908	63,500	Ford
1909	123,990	Ford
1910	181,000	Ford
1911	199,319	Ford
1912	356,000	Ford
1913	461,500	Ford
1914	548,139	Ford
1915	895,930	Ford
1916	1,525,578	Ford
1917	1,745,792	Ford
1918	943,436	Ford
1919	1,651,625	Ford
1920	1,905,560	Ford

NOTE: In 2014 there were 4,253,200 domestic passenger cars produced in the United States. General Motors was the top U.S. producer of passenger cars.

Registered Automobiles in the U.S. and Estimated Total Population, 1900–1920

Year	Registered Automobiles	Total Population
1900	8,000	76,094,134
1901	14,800	77,585,128
1902	23,000	79,160,196
1903	32,920	80,632,152
1904	54,590	82,164,974
1905	77,400	83,819,666
1906	105,900	85,436,556
1907	140,300	87,000,271
1908	194,400	88,708,976
1909	305,950	90,491,525
1910	458,377	92,406,536
1911	618,727	93,867,814
1912	901,596	95,331,300
1913	1,190,393	97,226,814
1914	1,664,003	99,117,567
1915	2,332,426	100,549,013
1916	3,367,889	101,965,984
1917	4,727,468	103,413,743
1918	5,554,952	104,549,886
1919	6,679,133	105,062,747
1920	8,131,522	106,466,420

NOTE: In 2015 there were approximately 257,900,000 cars and light trucks registered in the United States. (No statistic for cars only is available.) The estimated total population of the U.S. in 2015 was 321,773,631.

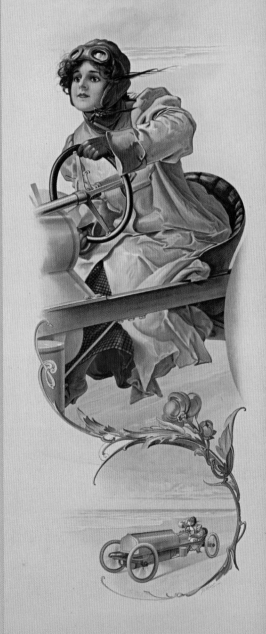

Above: **A racing poster from 1908**

Resources

BOOKS

Bausum, Ann. *With Courage and Cloth: Winning the Fight for a Woman's Right to Vote.* Washington, DC: National Geographic, 2004.
Auto tours were only a small part of the struggle for women's suffrage in the United States. Find out here about the challenges, triumphs, heroines, and villains in the seven-decade fight.

Editors of Consumer Guide. *The American Auto: Over 100 Years.* Lincolnwood, Illinois: Publications International, 2010.
This visual history includes a running time line featuring developments in the automotive industry, as well as hundreds of images of cars.

McConnell, Curt. *"A Reliable Car and a Woman Who Knows It": The First Coast-to-Coast Auto Trips by Women, 1899–1916.* Jefferson, North Carolina: McFarland and Company, 2000.
There's a lot to discover in this detailed study of five early cross-country automobile trips by women.

A woman drives a Buick in 1907.

Mitchell, Don. *Driven: A Photobiography of Henry Ford.* Washington, DC: National Geographic, 2010.
Written for a younger audience, this beautiful biography explores the life of the brilliant but complicated automotive pioneer.

Nystrom, Elsa A. *Mad for Speed: The Racing Life of Joan Newton Cuneo.* Jefferson, North Carolina: McFarland and Company, 2013.
With input from the subject's family members, Nystrom documents the life of America's first female auto racing star.

Scharff, Virginia. *Taking the Wheel: Women and the Coming of the Motor Age.* New York: The Free Press, 1991.
This is the definitive study of women and the motor car during the early twentieth century, full of fascinating observations and insights.

WEBSITES

America on the Move
amhistory.si.edu/onthemove/exhibition/exhibition_1_1.html
Covering more than 125 years, this online exhibit from the Smithsonian Institution's National Museum of American History documents the impact of the stagecoach, railroad, automobile, and several other types of transportation on American life.

Cyberspace Museum of Early American License Plates
mooj.com/PL8S.htm
Wondering what an Idaho license plate looked like in 1918? Check out this site, which shows the plates collected by one man covering 1903 to 1950.

National Association of Automobile Museums: Museum List
naam.museum/museum-list
Check here if you'd like to visit an automobile museum near you. At last count 36 states were represented, with more than 100 museums in all.

Old Car Advertisements
oldcaradvertising.com
Browse through ads from more than 75 car manufacturers going back as far as 1901 on this entertaining website.

PLACES TO VISIT

Auburn Cord Duesenberg Automobile Museum
1600 South Wayne Street
Auburn, Indiana 46706

automobilemuseum.org
This museum is a real "Duesy," the adjective meaning "the finest of its kind," borrowed from the Duesenberg automobile. It houses an awe-inspiring collection of hand-painted automobiles from three brands favored by the pre–World War II Hollywood elite.

The Henry Ford
20900 Oakwood Boulevard
Dearborn, Michigan 48124

thehenryford.org
Consisting of the Henry Ford Museum, the Greenfield Village outdoor museum, the Ford Rouge Factory Tour, and the Benson Ford Research Center, this complex will inspire the imagination of anyone interested in American—and especially transportation—history. There's easily a full day of fun to be had; more if you spend time looking at documents and artifacts in the Benson Ford archives.

Sources of Quotes

Throughout this book, the sources of display quotes appear with those quotes. Here are the sources of all the other quotations in the book, as well as the tables in the "Shifting Gears" Appendix. A full citation is given the first time a source is mentioned. After that, the citation is abbreviated.

CHAPTER 1
America, Meet the Motor Car

p. 11: "The United States...and Chicago." "Prize for Motors," *Chicago Times-Herald*, July 9, 1895, p. 1.

p. 17: "For private use...required." "The Motocycle Contest," the *Advocate*, December 18, 1895, p. 6.

p. 18: "in every...store." "Twelve Reasons: Gasoline, Steam, or Electricity?" *Motor*, April 1904, p. 24.

p. 19: "strong, durable...to drive," "the minimum...results," and "greater...horse." ibid.

p. 21: "We build...can make them." Henry Ford with Samuel Crowther, *My Life and Work* (Garden City, NY: Doubleday, Page and Company, 1922), p. 11.

p. 22: "The question of...to say the least." *Scientific American*, July 22, 1899, p. 69, quoted in "The Automobile and American English," by Theodore Hornberger, *American Speech*, April 1930, p. 274; "largely weeded out...percentage." "Terminology," the *Horseless Age*, June 7, 1899, pp. 5–6; and "The greatest need...will go." Henry Ford, "Arranging to Build 20,000 Runabouts" (letter to the editor), *Automobile*, January 11, 1906, p. 107, quoted in "The Road to the Model T: Culture, Road Conditions, and Innovation at the Dawn of the American Motor Age," by Christopher W. Wells, *Technology and Culture*, July 2007, p. 518.

p. 23: "I am like...with you." Letter From Lillian L. Sheridan to Henry Ford, January 21, 1922, in Henry Ford Office Accession, Jan.-June 1922, Box 46, at Benson Ford Research Center, Dearborn, MI; "the first...known here." "Makes Mark as Saleswoman in Seattle," *Ford News*, June 22, 1922, p. 7; "I just love...they pay." "Miss Sheridan Joins Baird in Selling of Fords," *Seattle Daily Times*, October 3, 1920, p. 42.; and "Mr. Phillips... design." "Says Men Cannot Beat Women in Sales Field," *Seattle Daily Times*, June 22, 1924, p. 37.

FEATURE 1
Motoring Laws

p. 27: "a person of mature age," "Nuisances on Highways, Section 3526," the *Vermont Statutes, 1894* (Rutland, VT, the Tuttle Company, 1895), p. 634; and "No person...following." *In Re Berry*, 147 Cal. 523, 82 p. 44 (1905).

CHAPTER 2
The Time of Her Life

p. 29: "not trained...to act quickly." "Public Opinion: Women and Motor Cars," by Montgomery Rollins, the *Outlook*, August 7, 1909, pp. 859–860.

pp. 30–31: "Woman was not...attempt it." "Do Women Make Good Drivers? A Woman's View," by Jennie Davis, *Motor*, May 1914, p. 62.

pp. 31, 33: "In my opinion...lose her head." "Against Women Autoists," *New York Times*, September 3, 1915, p. 9.

p. 33: "Nine out of...established." "Woman at the Motor Wheel," by Mrs. A. Sherman Hitchcock, *American Homes and Gardens*, April 1913, p. vi.

p. 34: "My wife...as I." "Another Word on the Tire Question," by Roger C. Aldrich, the *Horseless Age*, February 1, 1905, p. 149.

p. 35: "Learning to handle...marooned." "The Commuter's Wife and the Motor Car," by Christine McGaffey Frederick, *Suburban Life*, July 1912, pp. 13, 46; and "His real reason...would wish." "Woman at the Motor Wheel," by Mrs. A. Sherman Hitchcock, op. cit.

p. 36: "radially-swinging arm." "Window-Cleaning Device," patent # 743,801 by Mary Anderson of Birmingham, Alabama, November 10, 1903, accessed at https://docs.google.com/ viewer?url=patentimages.storage .googleapis.com/pdfs/US743801.pdf on August 26, 2015.

p. 37: "for your bride-to-be...safety." Quoted in Virginia Scharff, *Taking the Wheel: Women and the Coming of the Motor Age* (NY: The Free Press, 1991), p. 38; and "The smell...the electric." "My Lady of the Car," by Minna Irving, *Suburban Life*, November 1909, p. 233.

p. 38: "Dealers handling...deciding vote." "Automobile Builders Are Striving to Suit Women," the *Tennessean*, August 9,

1914, p. 29; and "So far as...the time of her life." H. Clifford Brokaw and Charles A. Starr, *Putnam's Automobile Handbook: The Care and Management of the Modern Motor-Car* (NY: G.P. Putnam's Sons, 1918), p. 303.

CHAPTER 3
Going the Distance

p. 42: "born mechanical." Alice Huyler Ramsey, *Veil, Duster, and Tire Iron* (Pasadena, CA: Castle Press, 1961), p. 11.

p. 43: "a quartet of nuns." ibid., pp. 3–4.

p. 47: "the driving...woman." "Women Have a New York-Philadelphia Endurance Run," the *Automobile*, January 14, 1909, p. 125; "There was only...out of it." "Transcontinental Automobile Trip," the *Hackensack Republican*, August 19, 1909, p. 1; and "I admit...journey." ibid., p. 8.

p. 48: "no fewer...visa versa." "Ocean-to-Ocean Trails Well Worn," *Motor*, December 1915, p. 56.

p. 49: "We took...the route." "Mrs. McCulloch Outlines Plan," *Chicago Daily Tribune*, November 12, 1910, p. 7.

pp. 49, 51: "No doubt...the state." "Equal Suffrage Missionaries," *Chicago Daily Tribune*, July 2, 1910, p. 6.

p. 51: "one of...victory." quoted in Scharff, op. cit, p. 80.

p. 52: "We are...journey." "A Symbolic Crew of Suffragists," *Lincoln Daily Star*, October 28, 1915, p. 7.

CHAPTER 4
The Need for Speed

p. 57: "O Mrs. Cuneo...uney O." Song quoted in "Eighth Day: Albany, N.Y., to Boston," by J.C. Wetmore, *Motor Age*, July 23, 1908, p. 11; "It was a case... around one." "A Woman's Automobile Racing Record," by Joan Newton Cuneo, *Country Life in America*, November Mid-Month, 1910, p. 127; and "Slow down!" "What a Woman Can Do With an Auto," by Robert Sloss, *Outing*, April-September, 1910, p. 68.

p. 59: "won more...woman alive." ibid., p. 64; and "marvelous riding qualities" Renault advertisement, *Automobile Topics Illustrated*, October 8, 1910, p. 72.

p. 61: "The rule...participating." "Woman Motorist To Race," *Salt Lake Herald*, June 10, 1904, p. 6; and "Chivalry...its place." "Mme. du Gast Seeks American Fame," by Monsieur Carbureter, *Motor*, May 1904, p. 16.

p. 62: "simple and understandable... experts." Dorothy Levitt, *The Woman and the Car: A Chatty Little Handbook for All Women Who Motor or Who Want To Motor* (London: John Lane, 1909), p. vi; and "to occasionally...behind you." ibid., p. 29.

p. 64: "the fastest...ever made." "Flares and Flickers," *Oregon Statesman*, November 21, 1920, p. 7; and "It is the most...can be driven." "Movie Men Stamp Approval on Essex Motion Picture Story," *San Francisco Chronicle*, February 15, 1920, p. 5.

p. 65: "Should Cuneo meet...in the contest." "Social Gossip," *Washington Post*, January 14, 1908, quoted in Elsa A. Nystrom, *Mad for Speed: The Racing Life of Joan Newton Cuneo* (Jefferson, NC: McFarland and Company, 2013), p. 128.

p. 67: "drove her own car...same circumstances." "Stories of the Photoplays," *Washington Herald*, July 22, 1914, p. 6; and "Woman is on a par... the experience." "Something New," the Doctors House Victorian Museum Presents the Nell Shipman Exhibit. glendaleca.gov/visitors/nell-shipman-doctor-house/something-new accessed January 25, 2016.

FEATURE 4
Road Reads

p. 69: "telling...lads." Clarence Young, *The Motor Boys* (NY: Cupples and Leon Co., 1906), p. v; "four healthy...does not." Ads for The Auto Boys series in Victor St. Clair, *Break O'Day Boys* (Akron, OH: The Saalfield Publishing Co., 1908); "There is no room...penned for girls." Ad for the Automobile Girls series in Laura Dent Crane, *The Automobile Girls at Washington* (Philadelphia, PA: Henry Altemus Company, 1913); "in the final... girls." Jacket blurb for *Motor Girls; or, A Mystery of the Road*, 1910, quoted in "Mobile Heroines: Early Twentieth-Century Girls' Automobile Series," by Nancy Tillman Romalov, *Journal of Popular Culture*, Spring 1995, p. 233; and "Billie Campbell...Motor Maid." Ad for the Motor Maids series in Katherine Stokes, *The Motor Maids by Rose, Shamrock & Thistle* (NY: Hurst and Company, 1912).

CHAPTER 5
Driving for Liberty

p. 71: "I was the...past my head." Mary Dexter, *In the Soldier's Service: War Experiences of Mary Dexter, England. Belgium, France, 1914-1918* (Boston, MA: Houghton Mifflin Company, 1918), p. 183.

p. 72: "always behaved...flattered." Gertrude Stein, *The Autobiography of Alice B. Toklas*, Chapter 6: The War, accessed online on February 10, 2016, at https://ebooks.adelaide.edu.au/s/stein/gertrude/toklas/chapter6.html.

p. 74: "crusader of mercy...Can you imagine it?" "Crusaders of Mercy," by Nancy Woods Walburn, *Motor*, May 1918, quoted in "Many Women Aid Near Trenches: Are Called 'Crusaders of Mercy,'" Oakland *Tribune*, May 5, 1918, p. 54; and "a national...sure victory." "The National League for Woman's Service," by Mrs. Coffin Van Rensselaer, *Annals of the American Academy of Political and Social Science*, September 1918, p. 282.

p. 75: "safe for democracy." Woodrow Wilson's speech to Congress, April 2, 1917, accessed February 13, 2016, at historymatters.gmu.edu/d/4943/; and "It was the first...every angle." Mrs. Coffin Van Rensselaer, op. cit. p. 275.

p. 76: "it has...a revolution." "The Automobile in War," the *Lotus Magazine*, November 1915, p. 79.

p. 77: "The organizers...much-needed men." Mrs. Coffin Van Rensselaer, op. cit. p. 281; and "We cover...intensive." "Women Drivers Form Motor Corps To Aid Nations in War," *New York Sun*, August 5, 1917, p. 45.

pp. 78, 80: "the first time...long distance deliveries." "Women Now Drive Big Motor Trucks," *New York Times*, April 28, 1918, p. 63.

p. 79: "the surprise and joy...cheer them." "100,000 Men in Uniform Entertained by World's Only Colored Motor Corps," *Philadelphia Tribune*, August 9, 1919, p. 1.

p. 81: "The only thing...anything else." "Women's Motor Corps of America," the [Marine Corps] *Recruiter's Bulletin*, January 1918, p. 15.

p. 82: "Fearless of the possibility... refused." "Motor Corps Activities," the *Red Cross Bulletin*, January 19, 1920, p. 2.

EPILOGUE
Bumpy Roads

p. 86: "We did not...the highways." Charles Coolidge Parlin and Fred Bremier, *The Passenger Car Industry: Report of Survey* (Philadelphia, PA: The Curtis Publishing Company, 1932), p. 87; "In the War...seclusion," ibid., p. 92; and "Modern housewives...their own," ibid., p. 21.

p. 87: "One of the first...look well in it?" Quoted in Regina Lee Blaszczyk, *The Color Revolution* (Cambridge, MA: MIT Press, 2012), p. 115.

pp. 87–88: "made me feel...to a man." "As the Woman Buyer Sees You," by Edith M. Garfield, *Motor*, January 1925, quoted in Scharff, op. cit. p. 127.

APPENDIX
Shifting Gears

p. 90: Requirements for Girl Scout Automobiling merit badge, 1916: Juliette Low, *How Girls Can Help Their Country*, Adapted from Agnes Baden-Powell and Sir Robert Baden-Powell's Handbook (NY: Girl Scout National Headquarters, 1916); for Total Cars Produced: Bureau of the Census, "Motor Vehicles—Production, Registrations, and Motor Fuel Usage, 1900-1945" in *Historical Statistics of the United States, 1789-1945* (Washington, DC: U.S. Department of Commerce, 1949), p. 223; for Top U.S. Car Producer: Editors of Consumer Guide. *The American Auto: Over 100 Years* (Lincolnwood, IL: Publications International: 2010); for footnote: "Passenger Car Production in the United States from 1999 to 2014," The Statistics Portal accessed March 1, 2016, at statista.com/statistics/198482/us-passenger-car-production-since-1999/ and "Leading Passenger Car Manufacturers Worldwide in 2014," The Statistics Portal accessed March 1, 2016, at statista.com/statistics/198524/15-leading-passenger-car-manufacturers-worldwide.

p. 91: For table: Bureau of the Census, "Motor Vehicles—Production, Registrations, and Motor Fuel Usage, 1900-1945," ibid. and p. 26; for footnote: "Number of vehicles registered in United States, 2015," Hedges & Company accessed May 1, 2016, at https://hedgescompany.com/automotive-market-research-statistics/auto-mailing-lists-and-marketing; and "Population of the United States (2016 and Historical)," Worldometers accessed May 1, 2016, at worldometers.info/world-population/us-population.

Index

95

Photo Credits

Abbreviations used: Boise State University, Albertsons Library, Special Collections and Archives, Nell Shipman Papers: BSU; Collection of the Author: COA; Collections of The Henry Ford: THF; Library of Congress: LOC; Courtesy of the National Automotive History Collection, Detroit (Michigan) Public Library: DPL; National Geographic Partners: NGP; New York (New York) Public Library: NYPL.

Front cover (top and bottom), front flap, and back cover DPL; Case cover DPL; 1 Underwood Archives/Getty Images; 2–3 DPL; 4–5 DPL; 7 Courtesy of Danica Patrick; 8 Jackie Glasthal; 10–11 DPL; 12 (background) LOC, (inset) LOC LC-B2-584-3; 13 LOC Lot 2627, v. 5; 14–15 Division of Work & Industry, National Museum of American History, Smithsonian Institution; 15 Bettmann/Corbis; 16 COA; 19 COA; 20 Apic/Getty Images; 20–21 LOC LC-USZ62-14596; 22 Hulton Archives/Getty Images; 23 (background and inset) THF128591; 24 COA; 25 (top) Underwood Archives/Getty Images, (center) THF115643; 26 The Ram Tuli Collection; 26–27 LOC LC-H261-2095; 28–29 DPL; 30 Bettmann/Corbis; 31 Schomburg Center for Research in Black Culture, Photographs and Prints Division, NYPL; Courtesy of Madam Walker Family Archives/A'Lelia Bundles; 32 COA; 32–33 DPL; 33 Mark Jay Goebel/Getty Images; 34 DPL; 36 (background) US Patent & Trademark Office, (inset) Patrick Faricy/NGP; 37 (top) Schenectady Museum, Hall of Electrical History Foundation/Corbis, (center) Chuckstoyland.com; 38–39 Museum of the City of New York X2011.34.3700; 39 Bettmann/Getty Images; 40–41 National Motor Museum/Heritage Images/Getty Images; 42–43 DPL; 44 DPL; 45 (top) COA, (bottom) Special Collections, University of Vermont; 46 DPL; 46–47 DPL; 48 (map) Jon Bowen, National Geographic Maps, (bottom) DPL; 49 LOC LC-B2-2897-10; 50 DPL; 51 (both) Chicago History Museum/Getty Images; 52 (top) LOC National Woman's Party Records, (bottom) Universal History Archive/Getty Images; 53 COA; 54 (dog) Culture Club/Getty Images; 54–55 (women's and men's catalog pages) Art and Picture Collection, NYPL; 56–57 Bettmann/Corbis; 58 (both) DPL; 59 National Motor Museum/Heritage Images/Getty Images; 60 National Motor Museum/Heritage Images/Getty Images; 60–61 LOC LC-USZ62-100197; 62 Courtesy of Osprey Publishing, part of Bloomsbury Publishing PLC; 63 DPL; 64 BSU; 66 Art Media/Print Collector/Getty Images; 67 (top) LOC LC-B2-4248-7, (bottom) BSU; 68–69 (all) COA; 70–71 LOC LC-F8-6680; 72–73 Lt. Ernest Brooks/IWM/Getty Images; 73 From In the Soldier's Service by Mary Dexter; 74 LOC LC-B2-4711-7; 75 LOC POS-US.G52, no. 15; 76 The Miriam and Ira D. Wallach Division of Art, Prints and Photographs: Photography Collection, NYPL; 76–77 Edwin Levick/Getty Images; 78 THF99642; 79 Berenice Abbott/Getty Images; 80 War Department/Buyenlarge/Getty Images; 82–83 Rue des Archives/Granger, NYC; 83 Universal History Archive/Getty Images; 84 Tichnor Brothers Collection/Boston (Massachusetts) Public Library; 84–85 Gulfoil Historical Society; 85 Jim Heimann Collection/Getty Images; 87 COA; 88 Gavin Lawrence/Getty Images; 89 (background) Art and Picture Collection, NYPL, (theater) Helene Vallee/Vetta/Getty Images, (Daniels photo) Culture Club/Getty Images; 90 (badge) Marty Ittner, (car) LOC LC-USZ62-118747; 90–91 COA; 91 THF81758; 92 LOC LC-USZ62-22825.

Acknowledgments

This is one of those books that took a village to put together. I fear I would still be writing the manuscript today if not for the wisdom and guidance of my wonderful editor, Suzanne Fonda, the inspiring contributions of designer Marty Ittner, the knowing counsel of design director Jim Hiscott, and the (usually) gentle prodding of National Geographic's Paige Towler. I thank them, along with everyone else at National Geographic, especially my long-time editor, Jennifer Emmett.

Thanks also to Dr. Virginia Scharff, who encouraged me to write a book in the field she pioneered and then was kind enough to act as our consultant. I offer my appreciation as well to the librarians and archivists at the Benson Ford Research Center and the Library of Congress for helping me dig out the information and images I needed, and to Aaron Warkentin, curator of the Auburn Cord Duesenberg Automobile Museum, for guiding me through their exquisite collection. And finally, thanks to my family and friends for their ongoing patience and support.